The Official EPAKS Guide to Short Form One

© 2014 EPAKS Publications

Pompano Beach, FL USA

ISBN: 0-9769823-0-2

Publisher

EPAKS Publishing

Author

Ken Herman

Illustrations

Marc Wolpert

Ed Parker Jr.

Ken Herman

Cover Design

Marc Wolpert

Ken Herman

Proof Readers

Alexander Perez

Steven Saviano

Kit Herman

Anthony Ramirez

Special thanks to:

those who contributed their time and efforts toward the development of this publication. Your efforts are appreciated and were invaluable to its development. You should be proud.

Also, no EPAKS publication would be complete without a special thank you to the person who made this all possible - Senior Grand Master and founder of the American Kenpo system - Edmund Kealoha Paker Senior: You are greatly missed.

**In loving memory of our founder
SGM Edmund Kealoha Parker Senior
3/19/1931 - 12/15/1990**

Table of Contents

Chapter 1 - Introduction

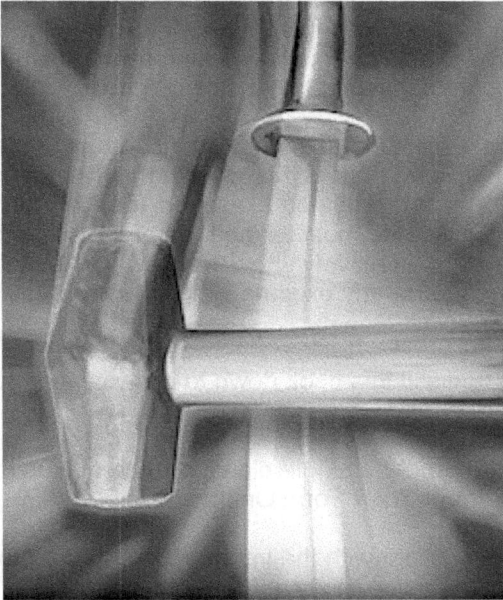

Short Form One is the foundation of all the forms in the American Kenpo system. Even though it has the least amount of moves and is the simplest to perform, it lays the foundation for each subsequent form.

Although Short Form One is the simplest form, one would be incorrect to assume that this implies that it is also the easiest form to perform. Because there are such few moves in the form, it is quite easy to spot errors, problems, physical quirks, inconsistencies, and/or misunderstood motion during the execution of this form.

Many senior instructors will ask a student newly introduced to them to perform this form for them. The purpose of this is to gauge and 'get a sense' as to the level of proficiency the practitioner has in the system. A well executed Short Form One shows a mastery of the physical and conceptual basics of the system. And, a poorly executed Short Form One shows either that the practitioner is lazy, uninformed, ill taught, or not patient enough to master such a simple form.

As a contrast - most experienced American Kenpoists will say and know that Form Four is the heart of the system for information and sophisticated execution. This is true. But, Short Form One is the most telling form of the system because it will quickly and effectively show the viewer whether the practitioner can properly execute simple basics and maneuvers.

If one were to distill this book down to its two major purposes, they would be:

1) To give the reader a single place to reference as much information about Short Form One as possible.

2) To help the reader with the information gathered to perform Short Form One as perfectly as possible.

Chapter 2 - History of Short Form One

The history of Short Form One is not entirely known. What is known is that the form existed in some manner prior to SGM Parker's influence to kenpo. Being that the form is not very complex - it can be surmised that it probably wasn't very different from today's version.

Prior to SGM Parker

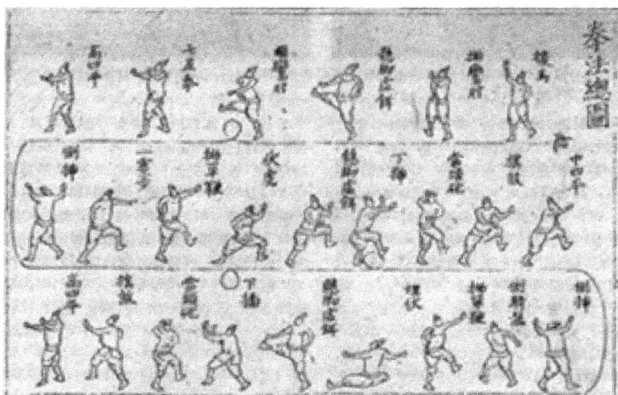

It is surmised that this form existed even prior to James Mitose and William K.S. Chow - SGM Parker's immediate forefathers. And, it is very probable and likely that this form existed in some manner or another as far back as the beginnings of kenpo - in B.C.E. times, in China.

During SGM Parker's Life

The Ed Parker's Basic Booklet

(Copyright 1967)
This was the first published explanation of Short Form One. It's
description included mainly the right side of the form, but also
gave a description of how to do the left side. It was very terse
in it's descriptions, illustrations, and information taught in the
form. But, it exposed the reader to a reference into Mr.
Parker's thoughts at a moderately early time in American
Kenpo's history.

The IKKA Belt Sheets / Manuals (Pasadena School)

(Copyright 1970)
The Pasadena school belt manuals were never published, but were handed out to students to be used during their classes and for personal study. They were essentially a list of the basics, forms, sets, etc. that were to be learned at a specific rank, prior to moving onto a new rank. Many organizations, schools, and teachers still use similar sheets / manuals for their students. Short Form One is listed in the Orange belt manual. Please keep in mind that at this time in American Kenpo history there was no yellow belt.

The IKKA Accumulative Journal Version 1.0

(Copyright 1972)
This was the second published explanation of Short Form One. It's description only included the right side of the form. This description was considered the standard until the publication of the Infinite Insight series.

The Infinite Insights into Kenpo - book #5

(Copyright 1987)
This was the third, and most comprehensive, explanation of Short Form One. It's description gave not only the physical and pictorial narration of this form, but the first written comprehensive analysis of this form. It also gave a written illustration of how to execute the second side of this form. This explanation is still considered by most to be the most widely read version of this form.

After SGM Parker's Death

The Encyclopedia of Kenpo

Version 1.0
(Copyright 1992)
This is the fourth published reference to Short Form One. The reference merely stated when the form should be taught (at yellow belt).

The IKKA Accumulative Journal

Version 2.0
(Copyright 1992)
This is the last, official written reference to Short Form One that can be somewhat attributed to SGM Parker's direct influence. It is an accumulation of revisions he was working on at the time of his death. It was compiled by his son Ed Parker Jr.

Chapter 3 - The Salutation and "Signifying"

In formal situations, the salutation and "signifying" are appended to the execution of a form. This practice adds clarity and formality to the form by allowing the viewer to not only determine the martial art style of the practitioner, but also the form which is intended to be performed; and whether the form will be modified from its standard execution.

The salutation is always appended to both the beginning and the end of the form. But, the signification gesture is only added to the beginning of the form.

The Salutation

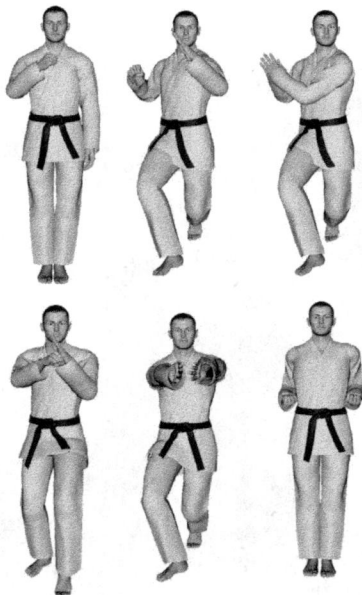

Original Salutation

The original Kenpo salutation dates back to the boxer rebellion in China. At that time, the salutation was used as a gesture to show that you where one of the individuals fighting to bring back the Ming dynasty. The left hand over right fist represented the sun and the moon, which in Chinese characters formed the symbol of the Ming dynasty.

However, the salutation as executed today by American Kenpo practitioners is longer than the original and now only represents a linkage to its past heritage of Kenpo. The reason the modern day salutation is longer than the original is that SGM Parker added a "new" series of maneuvers to the end of the original salutation. This change was to represent a merging of the modern martial arts with those of the past.

'new' addition to salutation

Salutation Standard Exection

Note:
> H = Horizontal - Example: 6:00H
> V = Vertical - Example 12:00V

___

Note:
> Throughout the salutation, the foot and hand maneuver timing should be synchronized such that both start and come to a complete stop simultaneously.

___

1) From an attention stance (toward 12:00H), bow and raise your head.
Meaning:
> Show respect to the art of kenpo.

___

2) Step sideways, with your left foot (toward 9:00H), into a meditating horse stance (toward 12:00H) while simultaneously placing your left hand folded over (on a 1:30V - 7:30V line) your right fist (on a 10:30V - 4:30V line) parallel to your body in front of you, at chin level.
Meaning:
> Foot Maneuvers:
>> I cast off the weak.
> Hand Maneuvers:
>> I hide my treasure

___

3) Bow your head into meditation.
Meaning:
> The meditation may vary depending upon the purpose of the salutation:
> Opening a Form:
>> The practitioner is to clear the mind of any external thoughts.

Closing a Form:
    The practitioner is to meditate on the execution
    performance of the form.

---

4)   Lift your head from meditation.
Meaning:
    You have finished meditation.

---

5)   Raise both of your hands above your head (toward
    12:00V), palms up (toward 12:00V), and without any loss
    of momentum draw your left foot (toward 3:00H) to your
    right foot while simultaneously lowering both of your hands
    in outward arches (left toward 9:00H - right toward 3:00H),
    ending into an attention stance (toward 12:00H).
Meaning:
    I draw the weak back to the strong.

Note:
    This is the point at which one would signify the form being
        performed.

---

6)   Step forward with your right foot (toward 12:00H) into a
    right front twist stance (toward 12:00H) while
    simultaneously bringing both your right clenched fist and
    left open hand over your right shoulder with your right fist
    facing forward (toward 12:00H) and your left palm facing
    over your right shoulder (toward 6:00H) covering your right
    fist.
Meaning:
    The scholar and the warrior meet...

---

7) Step forward, with your left foot (toward 12:00H) into a left
    45 degree cat stance (toward 12:00H) while
    simultaneously pushing both hands (maintaining contact
    with each other) forward (toward 12:00H) so your left open
    hand (palm facing downward (4:30V) and to your right
    toward 1:30H) covers your left side of fist (knuckles facing
    forward toward 10:30H) in front of you, at chin level.

Meaning:
    and go forth into battle,...

8) Rotate and open both of your hands (maintaining contact
    with each other), in opposite directions, so that both palms
    face away from each other (left toward 9:00H - right toward
    3:00H).

Meaning:
    back to back they will work together...

9) Step back (left rear cross-over) with your left foot (toward
    6:00H) into a right front twist stance (toward 12:00H) while
    simultaneously rotating both hands (still maintaining
    contact with each other) toward yourself, ending in a palm
    up position (toward 12:00V) in front of you at chin level.
    Draw your right foot back to your left foot (toward 6:00H)
    until both feet are side-by-side, while drawing and closing
    both hands simultaneously to chambered positions, palm
    up (toward 12:00V) at your sides, into a modified attention
    stance (toward 12:00H).

Meaning:
    to bring the country back to the people.

Note:
    Every move beyond this point was added by SGM Parker
    and is considered the "new" part of the salutation.

10) Step to your left with your left foot (toward 9:00H) into a horse stance while simultaneously raising both of your hands upward and in front of you (toward 12:00V) in slight outward arches, ending head high with palms away from you (toward 12:00H), while the thumbs and forefingers of both hands touch, forming a triangle [with the base of the triangle parallel to both the ground and your body (on a 9:00H - 3:00H line) and the tip of the triangle pointing straight upward (toward 12:00V)].

Meaning:
 I have no weapons.

---

11) Lower both hands (toward 6:00V) so your left folded over hand (on a 1:30V - 7:30V line) covers your right fist (on a 10:30V - 4:30V line) parallel to your body in front of you at chin level.

Meaning:
 I hide my kenpo treasure

---

12) Continue the drop of your hands (toward 6:00V), to solar plexus level, while opening both of your hands simultaneously so the palms face each other (left toward 3:00H - right toward 9:00H) touching with the fingers pointing straight upward (toward 12:00V), as if praying.

Meaning:
 I pray for forgiveness for having to use my karate.

---

13) Raise both of your hands above your head (toward 12:00V), palms up (toward 12:00V) and without any loss of momentum draw your left foot (toward 3:00H) to your right foot while simultaneously lowering both of your hands in outward arches (left toward 9:00H - right toward 3:00H), ending into an attention stance (toward 12:00H).

Meaning:
 Close of the salutation

---

14) Bow and raise your head.
Meaning:
    Show respect to the art of kenpo.

Salutation Standard Execution - Illustration

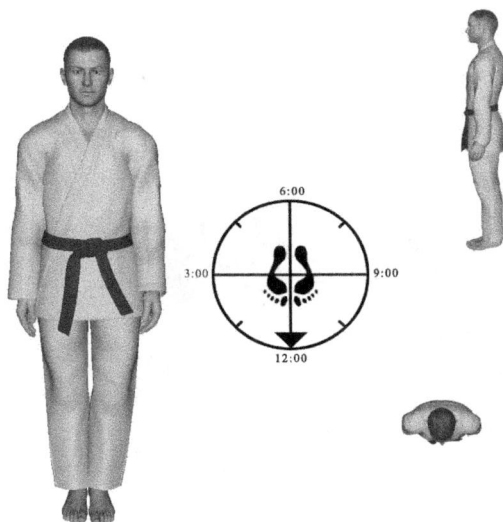

1) Opening Attention Stance

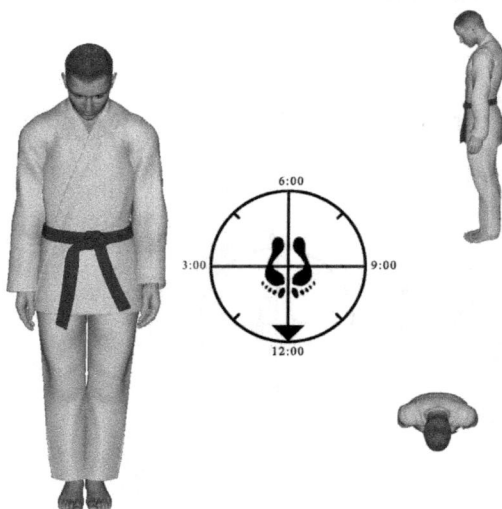

1b) Bow your head

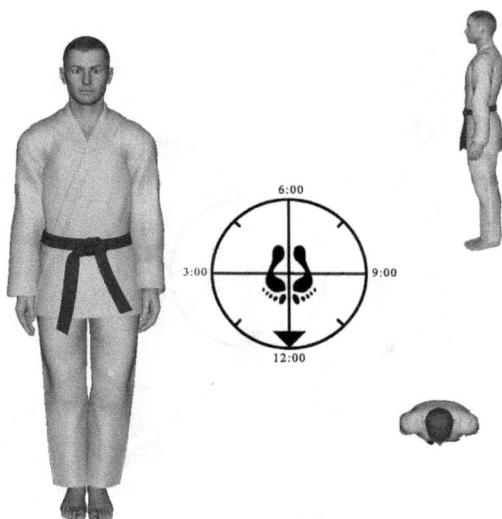

1c) Back to Attention Stance

2, 3 & 4) Meditating Horse

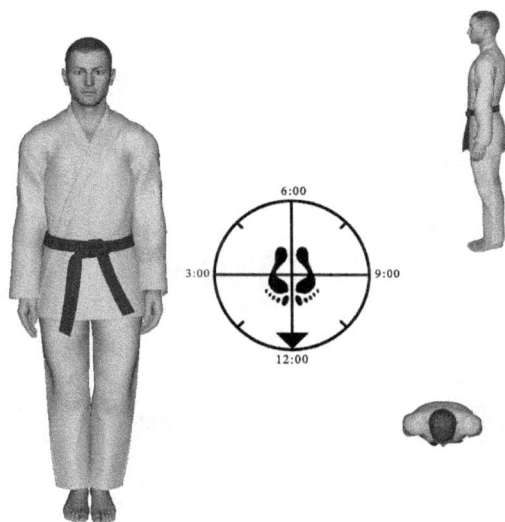

5) Back to Attention Stance

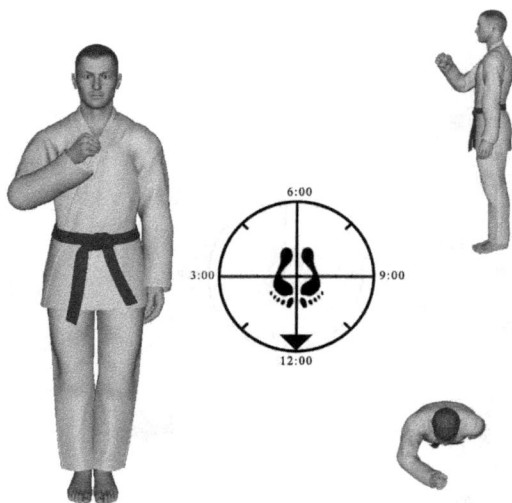

6a) the warrior

6b) and the scholar

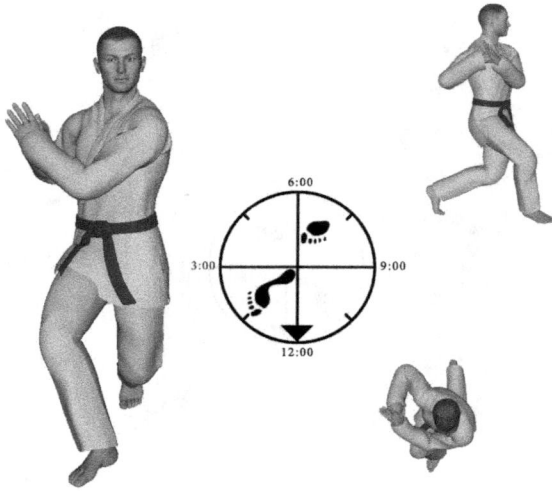

6c) meet

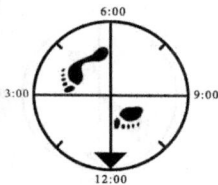

7) and go forth into battle

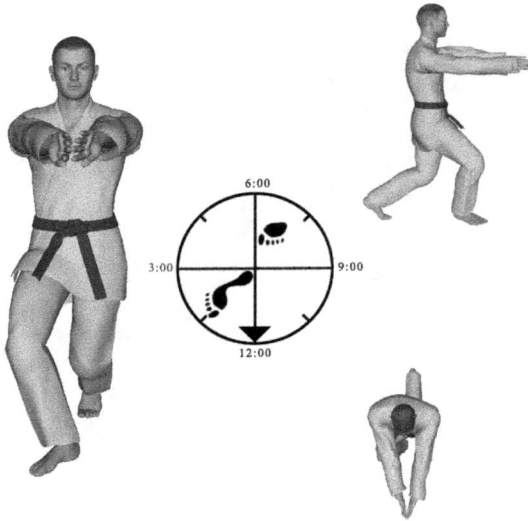

8) back to back they work

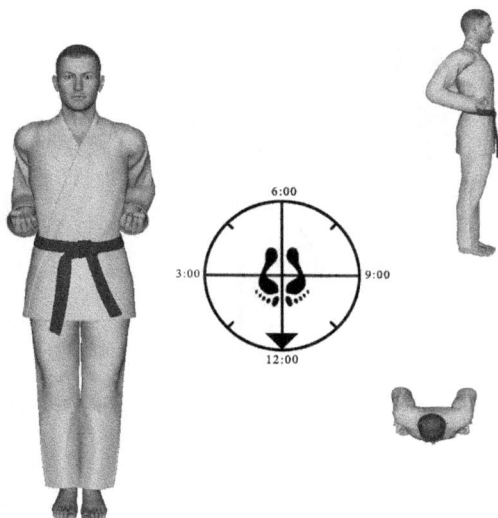

9) to bring the country back to the people

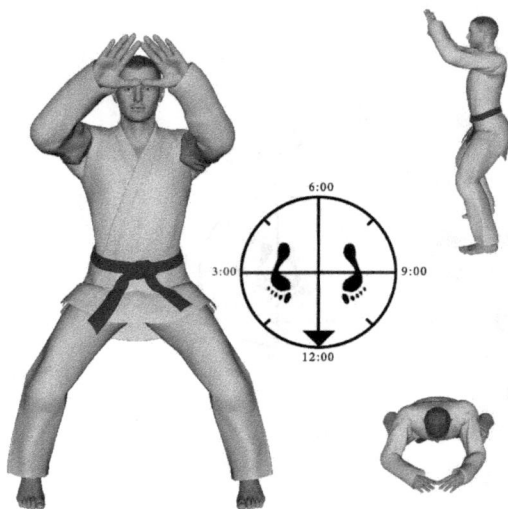

10) I have no weapons

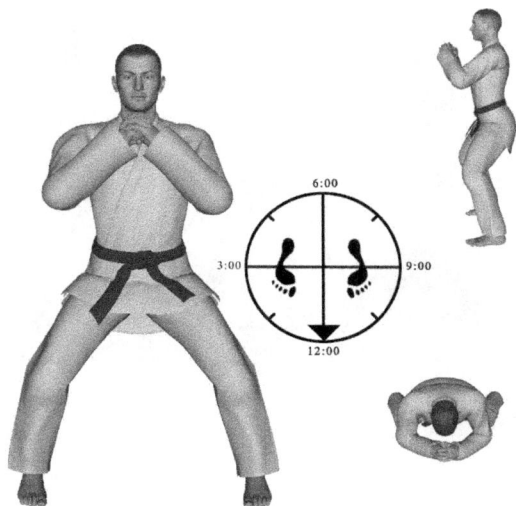

11) I hide my kenpo treasure

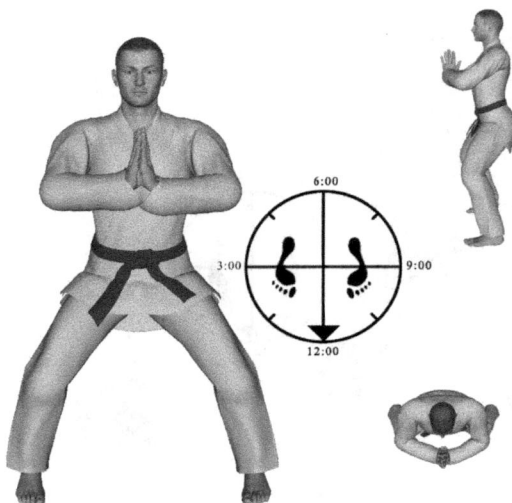

12) I pray for forgiveness
(for having to use my martial art)

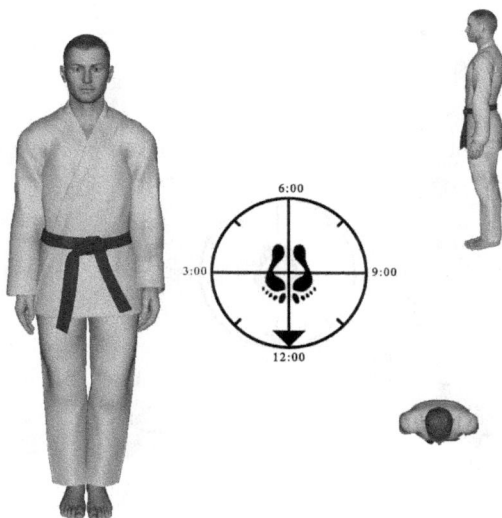

13) Back to Attention

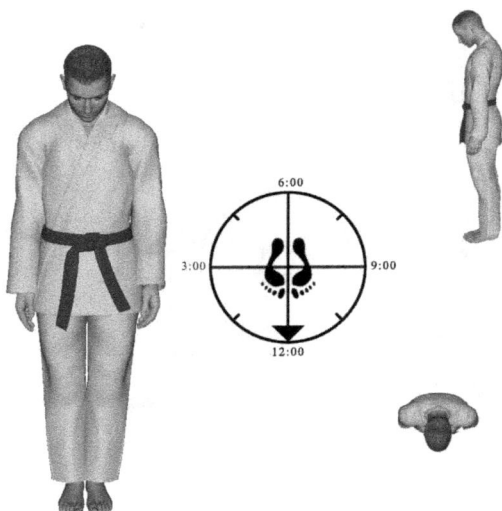

13a) Bow your head

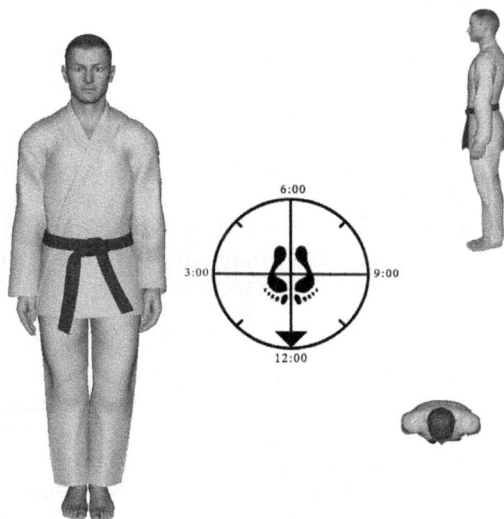

6:00

3:00

9:00

12:00

13b) Back to Attention

Salutation Variations

The first four forms (Short Form One, Long Form One, Short Form Two, Long Form Two) each start from a horse stance. Therefore, the salutation for each of these forms is generally executed up to the last meditating horse stance, without drawing back to the final attention stance. The form is then executed from that point in the salutation. But, if the practitioner draws back to the final attention stance, thus finishing the full salutation - they may simply step back into a horse stance, and continue the execution of the form from that point.

One other common variation is the period of time meditation is performed during the salutation. This length of time can be skipped or can last for as long as a few seconds - but generally not longer, unless needed. This meditation is provided for the practitioner, in order for them to become calm and focused in both body and mind. So meditation length will vary by individual.

"Signifying" a Form

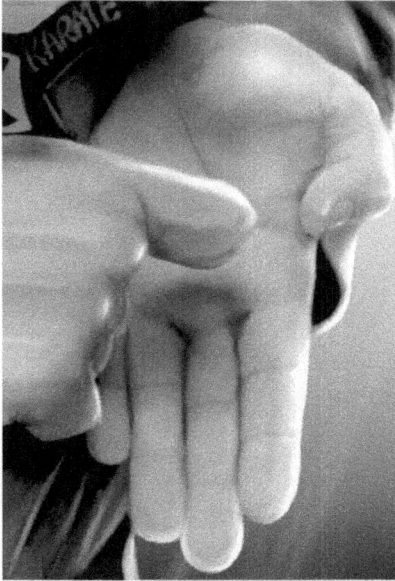

"Signifying" Short Form One

Signifying (or signing) is a hand gesture that is displayed prior to executing a form. In the case of Short Form One, the sign is a single finger (the index finger) bent in half and lay on top of the other opened hand (the backstop hand). This hand maneuver is typically done from an attention stance; displayed at waist level, facing front (i.e. perpendicular to the ground); and executed prior to the salutation. The backstop hand is positioned palm forward and fingers pointing to the ground. The signifying hand is placed perpendicular across the backstop hand, finger(s) pointing to the side, and palm facing the backstop hand.

The history of signifying a form comes from the early competition days (prior to the 1970's). At this time, the participant was not allowed to talk to the presiding judges. So, to inform the audience and judges as to which form was to be executed, the signification was added at the beginning. Also, the display was shown on both sides of the body, so as to cover a 180 degree radius.

"Signifying" with Salutation - Illustration

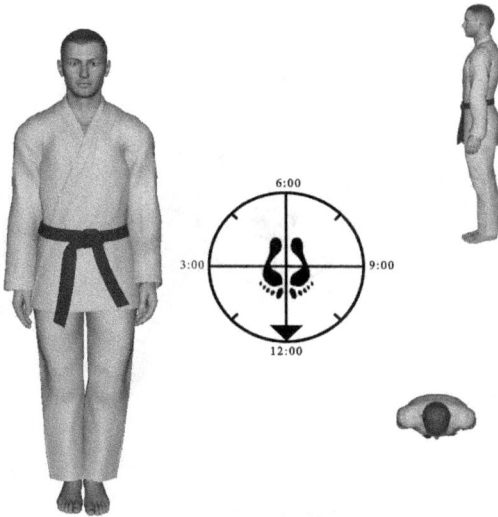

1) Opening Attention Stance

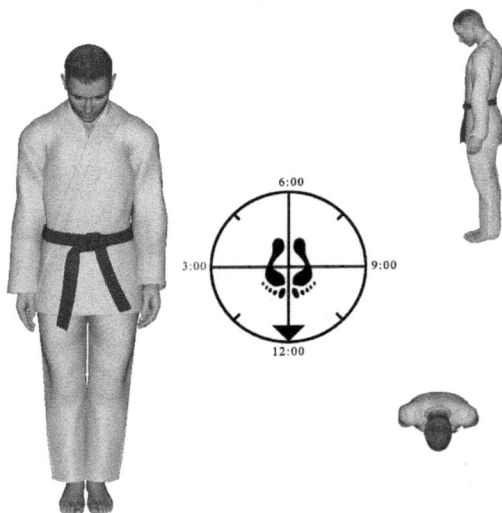

1b) Bow your head

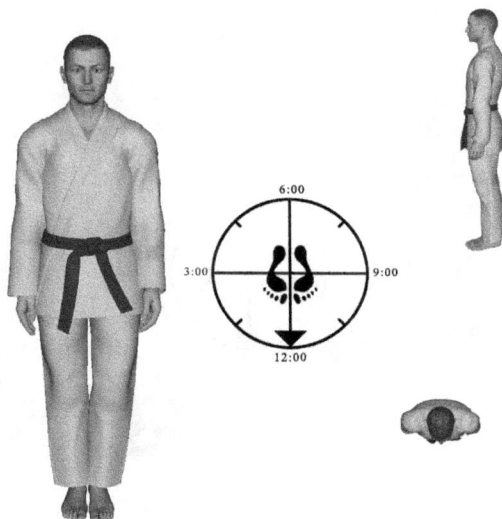

1c) Back to Attention Stance

2, 3 & 4) Meditating Horse

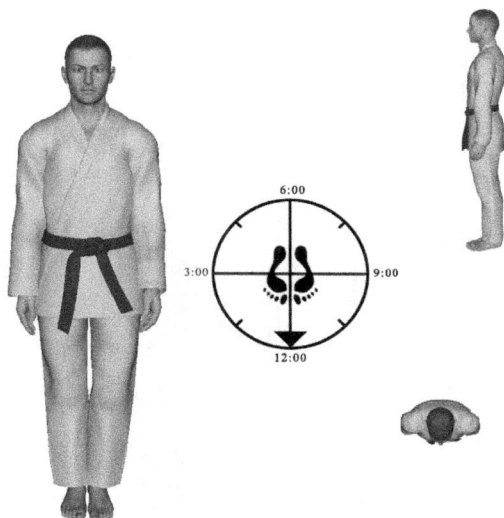

5) Back to Attention Stance

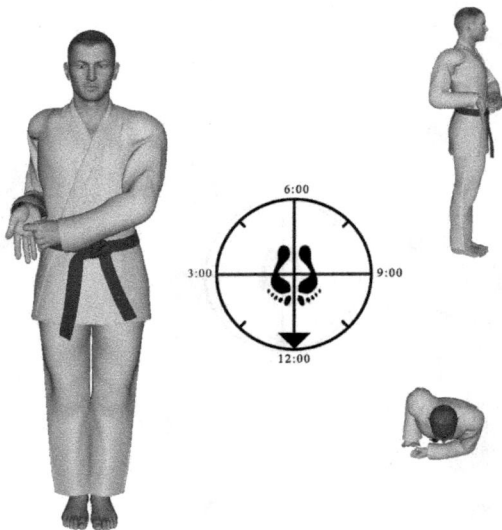

6) Signify on right side

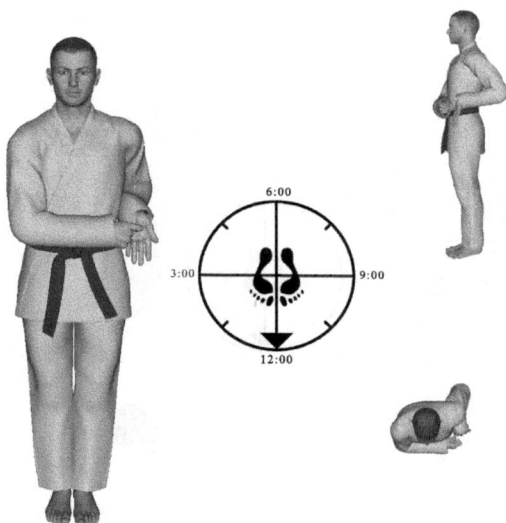

7) Signify on left side

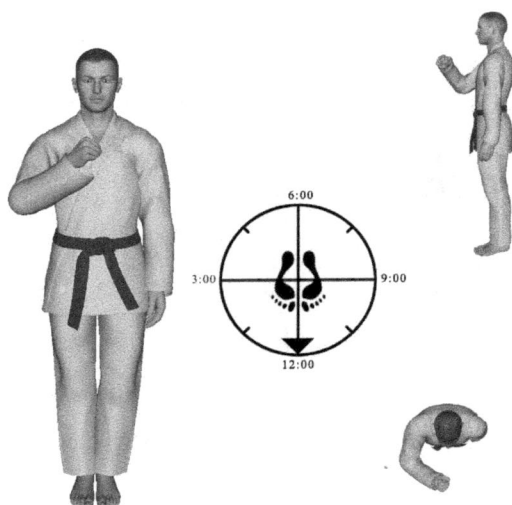

8a) the warrior

8b) and the scholar

8c) meet

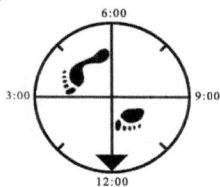

9) and go forth into battle

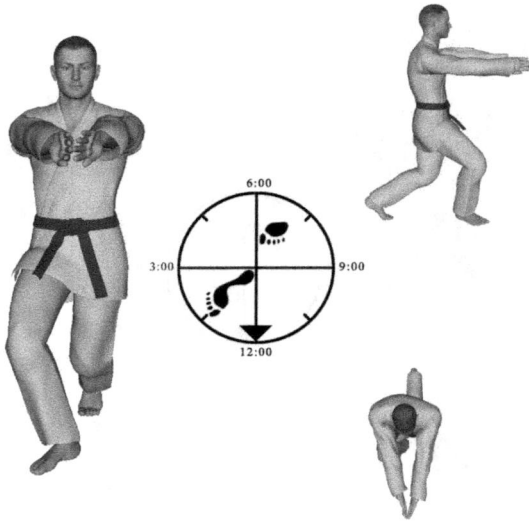

10) back to back they work

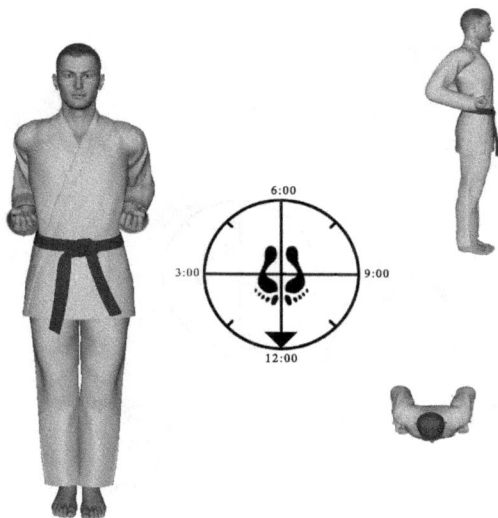

11) to bring the country back to the people

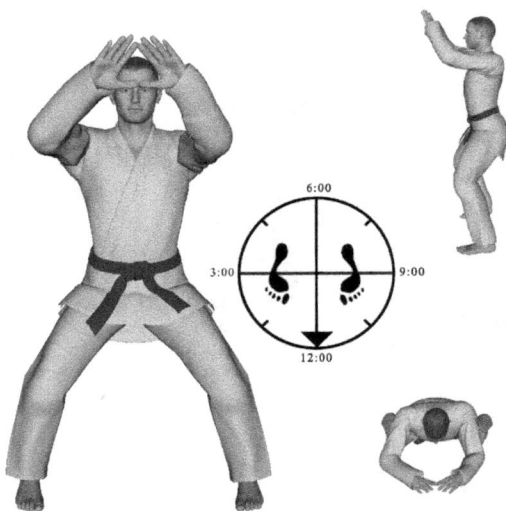

12) I have no weapons

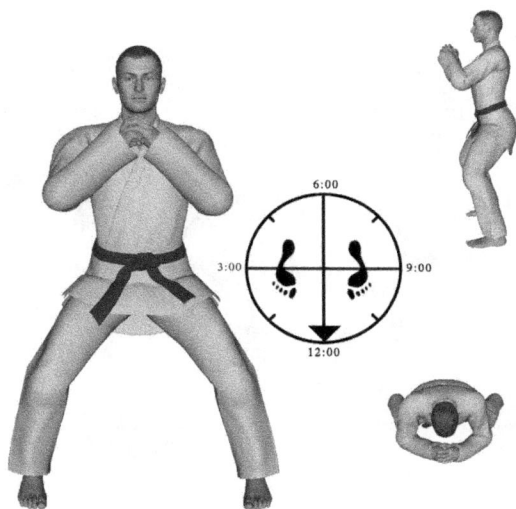

13) I hide my kenpo treasure

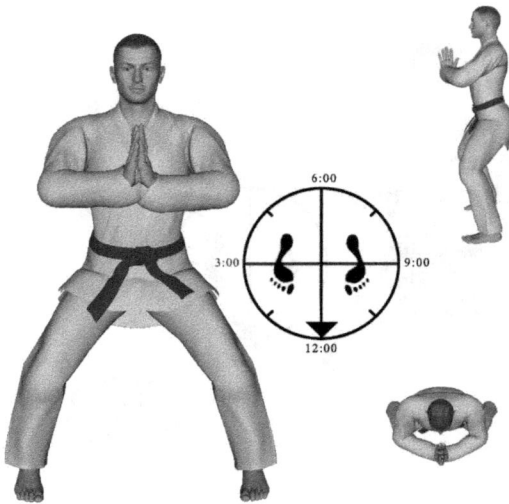

6:00

3:00

9:00

12:00

14) I pray for forgiveness
(for having to use my martial art)

15) Back to Meditating Horse

"Signifying" Variations

There are a number of variations to signifying that have appeared over time which have become part of the standard way of signifying a form. Some of the variations are widely used, some are not well known, but each of the variations is optionally applied as needed.

The first variation is whether the form is signified at all. At first, only the upper forms (short three and above) were signified and utilized the salutation. But over time, signifying and the salutation were considered appropriate for all forms (but typically not sets). An added benefit to adding the signification and salutation to the lower forms was that it made the forms a great deal longer and gave the form a greater feeling of complexity. If compared to Short Form One, the signification and salutation, at least, double the execution time and complexity of the form. Also, the signification and salutation are typically only executed in formal situations, such as competitions and tests; otherwise, a form is executed alone – either from the horse stance (the lower forms) or the attention stance (the upper forms).

The next variation is whether the signifying hand touched or hovered over the backstop hand. If the signifying hand was touching the backstop hand, this indicated that the form being executed was modified from the standard execution. But, if the signifying hand hovered over the backstop hand, this indicated that the form was to be executed without modification. The exceptions to this rule are the forms five and six. The forms five and six would always have the signifying hand touch the backstop hand.

Another variation is to signify on both sides of the body or just a single side. Signifying on a single side of the body indicated that the form would be executed on only that side. For instance, if the signification was only given on the right side, then only the right side of the form would be executed. But, if given on both sides of the body, then both the left and right side of the form would be executed. This variation is specifically indicative of Short Form One - which is commonly executed on both the right and left side for competition.

Chapter 4 - Execution of Short Form One

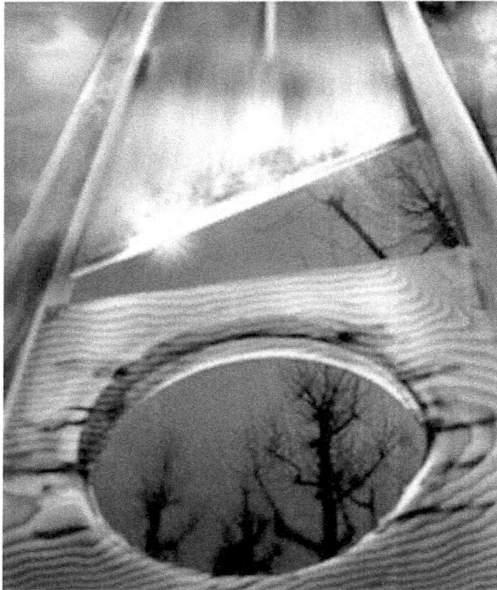

In this section, we will discuss the execution of Short Form One. The execution presented, for the purposes of this discussion, will be considered the standard execution of the form. All information about the form will be derived from this standard of execution. This does not mean there are not legitimate variations to this standard.

For instance, one of the most common variations to the form is to execute Short Form One on both the right and left side. The logic behind this typically stems from the fact that the left side picks up the opposite information of the right side. This is correct. But, execution of the left side is not necessary because the opposite information is presented in Long Form One - during the triple block section.

It is commonly thought that the left side was added to make the form longer for competition. Eight simple moves just wasn't long enough to compete with against other styles. Doubling the form still did not make it dynamic for open competition, but it did make the form longer. This change then filtered its way back into the studio, and became the "standard" way to execute the form - for that group and their lineage.

But, the reader should take note: The scenario presented above does not mean that executing both the right and left side is wrong. It just means that it is not necessary to the system. Executing the left side of Short Form One is redundant information as it relates to the system, not wrong information. Just as executing any form on the left side is possible, that does not mean it is necessary from a system standpoint.

Various "Standards"

As a general rule, all American Kenpo forms will have various "correct" ways of execution. This is due to a number of factors. But, each factor can be whittled down to one common and important characteristic, they each effect the "standard" execution of the form. Now, carry any of these change factors out a couple of instructor-to-student generations, and you get a resulting form with variations from the beginning of the cycle. But, each generation will swear that they do the form correctly. And, in their mind they are correct. Who is to say otherwise?

Why is the word "standard" in quotes in this section? Because standardization, as it relates to American Kenpo, can be a relative thing. Even Mr. Parker would change the execution of various forms for various reasons. Most of the time for one demonstration, but sometimes permanently.

For example, American Kenpo, as a style that we recognize today, was developed and evolved over a number of decades. During this time, SGM Parker got a large amount of feedback from a great number of direct and indirect students. Whenever he found feedback that was sound and reasonable, he would roll that feedback into his system. But, doing so would leave a number of students that were already taught the form with a slight variation from the now current "standard." Granted, this was infrequent, but it did happen.

Another reason for alternate "standards" of a form is that Mr. Parker would sometimes vary a form slightly while teaching it to a specific individual. This is called giving the form a signature. This practice was done so that when a new individual would come to Mr. Parker making claims as to their lineage, Mr. Parker could "test" the individual by having them perform a single or series of forms. From what he saw, SGM Parker could determine whether or not they were being truthful. With this knowledge, he could quickly determine the relative reliability of the individual. But, this practice has a serious side effect - the signature became a "standard." Why? Because that is how the practitioner learned the form from SGM Parker; and, the individual can correctly say that SGM Parker taught them to do the form that specific way. And, they are correct.

A third reason for a "standard" is the, "doesn't effect the information in the form" reason. This comes about because American Kenpo forms can be considered "books" of information about the system. But, certain moves and/or maneuvers can be altered slightly without information being lost or altered in the form. These changes are considered acceptable to the instructor, and as a new generation is taught the form, they will learn it slightly differently from the previous generation, generally without any information about the original version and reason for the change.

Probably the most common reason for a "standard" comes about from human error. The scenario goes like this: Mr. Parker teaches a student a form. The person goes home and practices the form, but forgets or accidentally varies the form in some way. But, they never get any further correction and/or feedback from SGM Parker about the "new" way of doing the form. They now teach it to a student with the change, each believing it is the correct and original way of executing the form. And, the cycle continues.

Form Standard Execution

Note:
>   H = Horizontal - Example: 6:00H
>   V = Vertical - Example 12:00V

From a meditating horse stance...

1

>   Step back with your left foot (toward 6:00H) into a right neutral bow (facing 12:00H) with a right hammering inward block (toward 10:30H) (major) while simultaneously retracting your left arm to a left chambered position, palm up (toward 12:00V).

2

>   a)
>   Draw your right foot toward your left foot (toward 6:00H) into a transitory right 45 degree cat stance (facing 12:00H) with a covering right inward block (toward 10:30H) (minor) while having your left arm remain in place.

>   b)
>   Without any loss of motion, step back, with your right foot (toward 6:00H) into a left neutral bow (facing 12:00H) with a left thrusting inward block (toward 1:30H) while simultaneously retracting your right arm to a right chambered position, palm up (toward 12:00V).

3

a)
Cover, with your right foot (toward 3:00H) (90 degrees) (counter clockwise), into a transitory left neutral bow (facing 9:00H) with a covering right thrusting inward block (toward 7:30H) (minor) while simultaneously retracting your left arm to a left chambered position, palm up (toward 12:00V).

b)
Settle into a left neutral bow (facing 9:00H) with a left thrusting vertical outward block (toward 6:00H) (major) while simultaneously retracting your right arm to a right chambered position, palm up (toward 12:00V).

4

a)
Draw your left foot toward your right foot (toward 3:00H) into a transitory left 45 degree cat stance (facing 9:00H) with a covering left hammering inward block (toward 10:30H) (minor) while having your right arm remain in place.

b)
Without any loss of motion, step back, with your left foot (toward 3:00H), into a right neutral bow (facing 9:00H) with a right thrusting vertical outward block (toward 12:00H) (major) while simultaneously retracting your left arm to a left chambered position, palm up (toward 12:00V).

5

a)
Cover, with your right foot (toward 6:00H) (180 degrees) (counter clockwise) into a transitory left neutral bow (facing 3:00H) with a covering right hammering inward block (toward 1:30H) (minor) while having your left arm remain in place.

b)
Settle into a left neutral bow (facing 3:00H) with a left thrusting upward block (toward 12:00V) (major) while simultaneously retracting your right arm to a right chambered position, palm up (toward 12:00V).

6

a)
Draw your left foot toward your right foot (toward 9:00H) into a transitory left 45 degree cat stance (facing 3:00H) with a covering left hammering inward block (toward 4:30H) (minor) while having your right arm remain in place.

b)
Without any loss of motion, step back, with your left foot (toward 9:00H), into a right neutral bow (facing 3:00H) with a right thrusting upward block (toward 12:00V) (major) while simultaneously retracting your left arm to a left chambered position, palm up (toward 12:00V).

7

a)
Cover, with your left foot (toward 12:00H) (90 degrees) (clockwise) into a transitory right neutral bow (facing 6:00H) with a covering left thrusting inside downward block (toward 9:00H), palm up (toward 12:00V) (minor) while simultaneously cocking your right arm horizontally across your waist (toward 3:00H), palm up (toward 12:00V).

b)
Settle into a right neutral bow (facing 6:00H) with a right hammering outside downward block (toward 9:00H) (major) while simultaneously retracting your left arm to a left chambered position, palm up (toward 12:00V).

8

a)
Draw your right foot toward your left foot (toward 12:00H) into a transitory right 45 degree cat stance (facing 6:00H) with a covering right thrusting inside downward block (toward 3:00H), palm up (toward 12:00V) (minor) while simultaneously cocking your left arm horizontally across your waist (toward 9:00H), palm up (toward 12:00V).

b)
Without any loss of motion, step back, with your right foot (toward 12:00H) into a left neutral bow (facing 6:00H) with a left hammering outside downward block (toward 3:00H) (major) while simultaneously retracting your right arm to a right chambered position, palm up (toward 12:00V).

9

Cover, with your left foot (toward 10:30H) (180 degrees) (clockwise) into a meditating horse stance (facing 12:00H) by placing your left open hand (on a 1:30V - 7:30V line) over your right fist (on a 10:30V - 4:30V line) parallel to your body in front of you at chin level.

Note:
The remaining part of this form, if executed, is the exact mirror image of the previously described steps.

10

Raise both of your hands above your head (toward 12:00V), palms up (toward 12:00V), and without any loss of momentum draw your left foot (toward 3:00H) to your right foot while simultaneously lowering both of your hands in outward arches (left toward 9:00H - right toward 3:00H), ending into an attention stance (toward 12:00H).

Closing salutation...

Form Standard Execution - Illustration

Note: The double factor blocks and associated transitory 45 degree cat stances are not illustrated in this section - even though they are expressly described in the 'Standard Execution' text. This is done purposely for the sake of simplicity.

Opening Meditating Horse

1) Right Hammering Inward Block

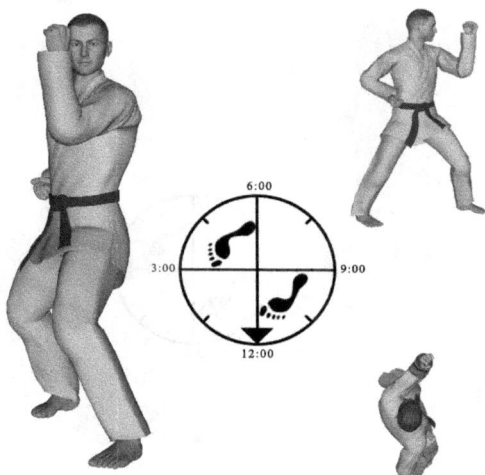

2) Left Thrusting Inward Block

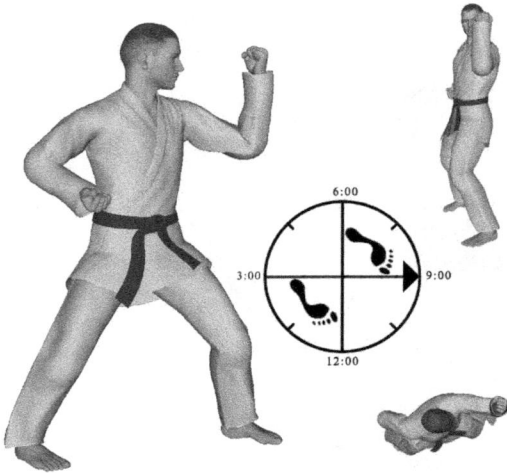

3) Left Vertical Outward Block

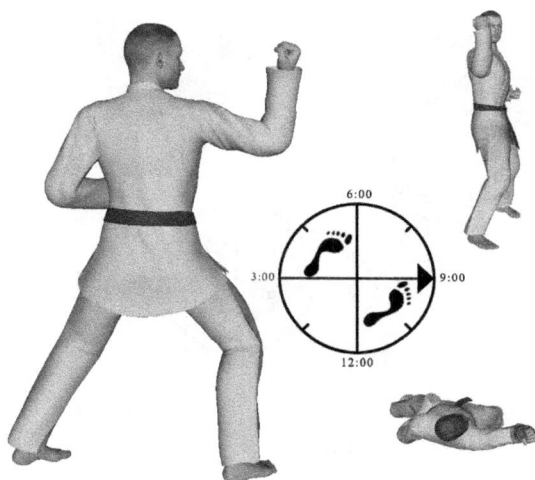

4) Right Vertical Outward Block

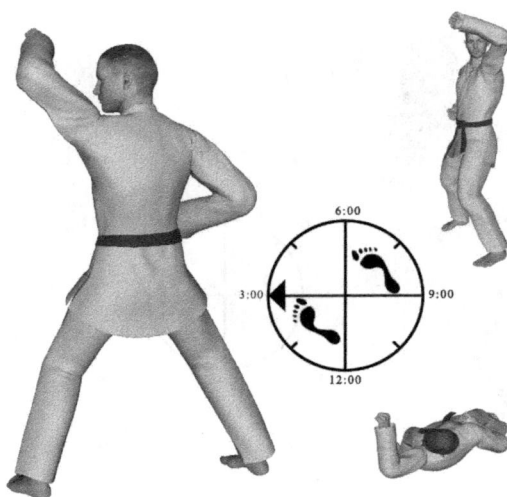

5) Left Upward Block

6) Right Upward Block

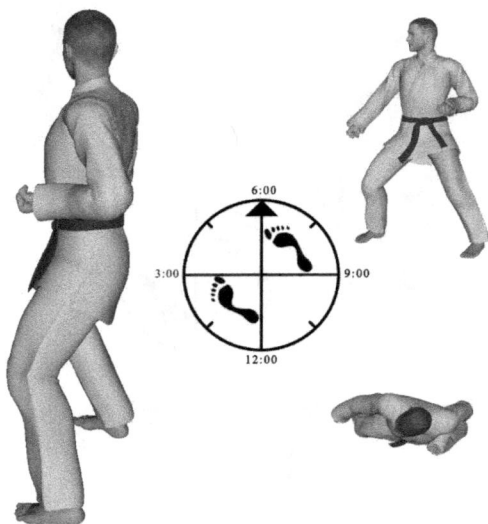

7) Right Downward Block

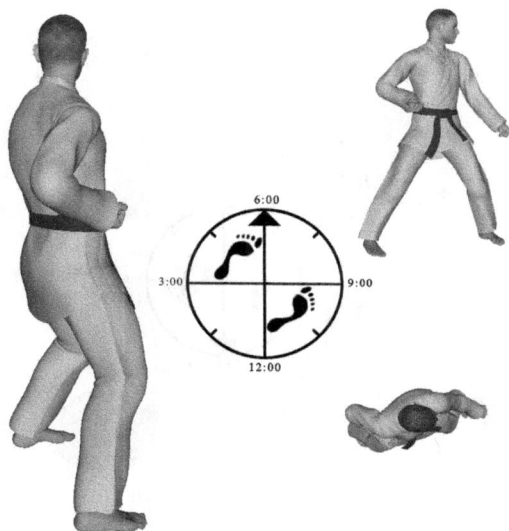

8) Left Downward Block

Closing Meditating Horse

Form Standard Execution - Video

EPAKS has produced a number of videos that have been uploaded to YouTube. The purpose of these videos is to demonstrate the execution of American Kenpo forms and self-defense techniques. They are not intended to be perfect. Instead, they are intended to be reasonably good examples of execution which the viewer can use as a benchmark. Among the videos is one demonstrating Short Form One. It may be viewed here:

https://www.youtube.com/watch?v=7CRgEIFaHIA

An example of American Kenpo Short Form One, Short Form 1

Chapter 5 - Understanding American Kenpo Forms

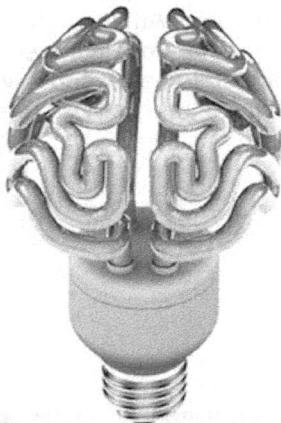

The most important thing to understand about an American Kenpo form is that it should not be thought of as an imaginary fight between the performer and (an) imaginary opponent(s). Many people make the assumption that is the way one must think about American Kenpo forms. This assumption comes from a couple of venues. For one, most self-defense systems structure their forms this way. For another, almost everyone visualizes an opponent in some way while executing their form. Visualization of an opponent is often used to focus strikes and maneuvers while also helping to provide psychological motivation. Also, visualization of an opponent is often used while learning and/or teaching a form.

In contrast to other styles of self-defense, American Kenpo forms are defined as:

> A predefined series of maneuvers that:
> 1) show the rules and principles of motion,
> 2) that everything has a reverse and an opposite,
> 3) by giving an example

Another way to look at it is: an American Kenpo form can be thought of as a packet of information, exposed as movement, used to convey some of the information that shapes the framework of the American Kenpo system. This information is to be learned along with the movements, thus continuing an unbroken line of succession from instructor to student.

One common way to begin to understand the information presented in American Kenpo forms is to first break the forms down into their respective categories. Through some simple analysis one of the first things that should to begin become apparent is that their appears to be three different types of forms. This appearance is correct. The name of the concept associated with this observation is called the Dictionary / Encyclopedia / Appendix analogy. Whereas dictionaries define individual words encyclopedias explain things and concepts in greater detail. But, appendices expand and expound upon a small or focused area of information. Using this explanation, one can create a one-to-one correlation to the observed three categories of forms.

The first four forms (the one's and the two's) appear to have a slightly different style than the higher forms. These forms fall into the 'dictionary' category. They are commonly referred to as defining motion. By this it is meant that these forms concentrate more on the basics and demonstrating their opposites and reverses, and less upon the concepts and theories.

The higher forms (the three's and up) appear to be far more complex than the lower forms. These forms fall into the 'encyclopedia' category. These forms, in contrast to the dictionary forms, lean more toward concentrating on the concepts and theories of American Kenpo and less towards the physical opposites and reverses.

The remaining type of form (the set) is very different from all the other forms. Sets are so different, in fact, that they even have a different name - i.e. sets. These forms fall into the 'appendix' category. By this it is meant that these forms have a very narrow scope. In other words, these forms concentrate and explore the information present within specific genre of information/motion.

Understanding Short Form One

So, how does Short Form One fit into the Dictionary / Encyclopedia / Appendix analogy?

First, Short Form One begins from a Meditating Horse stance. As a matter of fact, all forms up through Long Form Two begin from a Meditating Horse stance. Next, Short Form One starts with a Right, Hammering, Inward Block and sets an In / Out / Up / Down sequence. Again, all forms up through Long Form Two have the same properties. Therefore one can safely say: all Dictionary forms start from a Meditating Horse stance; begin with a Right, Hammering, Inward Block; and work on an In / Out / Up / Down sequence.

Next, Short Form One starts a foundation on which all of the rest of the Dictionary forms build. It introduces the concept of opposites (left / right, up / down, in / out, etc) and reverses (inward / outward, clockwise / counter-clockwise, direct rotational / counter rotational, etc). The important thing to notice about this foundation is that it is primarily focused on physical motion, not concepts.

As an example: an opposite to a right block is a left block - physical motions. Whereas an opposite to understanding is not understanding - a concept.

Chapter 6 - Basics of Short Form One

In order to properly analyze Short Form One, one must first become aware of all the basics that are employed in its execution. Since the first four forms (the one's and the two's) are considered the "dictionary" forms (i.e. they define motion), the emphasis on highlighting the basics is of greater significance than in the higher forms. In contrast, the higher forms (short 3 and above) tend to have more emphasis on theories and concepts over basics.

Also, by clarifying the utilized basics in Short Form One, one can begin to see its symmetry. Glancing at the "Quick Reference of Basics" section, one can quickly see that uniformity and consistency exists throughout the form. Each basic has its matching opposite. Nothing is left unmatched. This uniformity is important, because it sets the tone for analysis of the rest of the forms in the system. One should conclude that this symmetry is not by chance, but by design. SGM Parker was purposely meticulous in his design of the forms in American Kenpo.

The "Basics Utilized in Short Form One" section gives a more detailed analysis to each employed basic. This detail is provided to help in understanding the implementation and emphasis of each basic (by providing intent and method) and for remembering each step of the form (by providing direction, position, focus, and side). With this analysis, it is fairly straightforward to re-assemble the correct execution of Short Form One.

Quick Reference of Basics

Stances:
    Meditating Horse
    Neutral Bow (Right / Left)

Blocks (Major):
    Inward:
        Right (Hammering) / Left (Thrusting)
    Vertical Outward:
        Left / Right
    Upward:
        Left / Right
    Outside Downward (Palm Down):
        Right / Left

Blocks (Minor):
    Inward Double Factor:
        Right / Left
    Inside Downward (Palm Up) Double Factor:
        Left / Right

Foot Maneuvers:
    Step Through (Reverse):
        Left / Right
    Ninety Degree Cover:
        Right / Left
    One Hundred and Eighty Degree Cover:
        Right / Left

Basics Utilized in Short Form One

Presented in execution order

Stances	Side	Intent	Direction	Method/Area	Focus
Meditating Horse		Major			12:00H
Neutral Bow	Right	Major	Backward (6:00H)	Step Through (Reverse)	12:00H
Neutral Bow	Left	Major	Backward (6:00H)	Step Through (Reverse)	12:00H
Neutral Bow	Left	Major	Backward (3:00H)	90 degree Cover (Right)	9:00H
Neutral Bow	Right	Major	Backward (3:00H)	Step Through (Reverse)	9:00H
Neutral Bow	Left	Major	Backward (9:00H)	180 degree Cover (Right)	3:00H
Neutral Bow	Right	Major	Backward (9:00H)	Step Through (Reverse)	3:00H
Neutral Bow	Right	Major	Backward (12:00H)	90 degree Cover (Left)	6:00H
Neutral Bow	Left	Major	Backward (12:00H)	Step Through (Reverse)	6:00H
Meditating Horse		Major	Forward (12:00H)	180 degree Cover (Left)	12:00H

Blocks	Side	Intent	Direction	Position	Method/Area	Focus
Inward	Right	Major	Inward (10:30H)	Front	Hammering	12:00H
Inward	Left	Major	Inward (1:30H)	Front	Thrusting	12:00H
Inward	Right	Minor	Inward (7:30H)	Rear	Thrusting	9:00H
Vertical Outward	Left	Major	Outward (6:00H)	Front	Thrusting	9:00H
Inward	Left	Minor	Inward (10:30H)	Rear	Hammering	9:00H
Vertical Outward	Right	Major	Outward (9:00H)	Front	Thrusting	9:00H
Inward	Right	Minor	Inward (1:30H)	Rear	Hammering	3:00H
Upward	Left	Major	Upward (12:00V / 3:00H)	Front	Thrusting	3:00H
Inward	Left	Minor	Inward (4:30H)	Rear	Hammering	3:00H
Upward	Right	Major	Upward (12:00V / 3:00H)	Front	Thrusting	3:00H
Inside Downward (Palm Up)	Left	Minor	Inward (9:00H) / Downward (6:00V)	Rear	Thrusting	6:00H
Outside Downward (Palm Down)	Right	Major	Downward (6:00V) / Outward (9:00H)	Front	Hammering	6:00H
Inside Downward (Palm Up)	Right	Minor	Inward (3:00H) / Downward (6:00V)	Rear	Thrusting	6:00H
Outside Downward (Palm Down)	Left	Major	Downward (6:00V) / Outward (3:00H)	Front	Hammering	6:00H

Foot Maneuvers	Side	Intent	Direction	Focus
Step Through	Left	Major	Backward (6:00H)	12:00H
Step Through	Right	Major	Backward (6:00H)	12:00H
90 degree Cover	Right	Major	Backward (3:00H)	9:00H
Step Through	Left	Major	Backward (3:00H)	9:00H
180 degree Cover	Right	Major	Backward (9:00H)	3:00H
Step Through	Left	Major	Backward (9:00H)	3:00H
90 degree Cover	Left	Major	Backward (12:00H)	6:00H
Step Through	Right	Major	Backward (12:00H)	6:00H
180 degree Cover	Left	Major	Forward (12:00H)	12:00H

Chapter 7 - Analysis of Short Form One

In order to analyze Short Form One, One must first answer two simple questions:

1) What is it that is being analyzed?
2) What is the purpose of the analysis?

What is being analyzed?

The obvious answer is Short Form One is being analyzed. But what is Short Form One? In the most fundamental terms, Short Form One is a series of basics executed together to create a form. But, what is the purpose of creating a form? As mentioned earlier in this guide, American Kenpo forms are not to be thought of as a choreographed fight between the practitioner and (an) imaginary opponent(s) for demonstration purposes. American Kenpo forms are defined as:

A predefined series of maneuvers that:
1) show the rules and principles of motion,
2) that everything has a reverse and an opposite,
3) by giving an example

Provided with the above information, one can move on to the second question posed.

What is the purpose of the analysis?

Again, the obvious answer is to expose the information presented in Short Form One. But, what information is being exposed? From the definition derived above, one can limit their analysis to the three elements that compose the definition. Then, the major question that should now be asked is, "how will the exposed information be presented?"

The information exposed from Short Form One will be broken down into four sections:

Beginner / Intermediate Information

This section will summarize the information for which a beginner to intermediate practitioner should be aware. This is important because not all readers are advanced practitioners. This section will help them check what they know against what should be known about Short Form One – at the beginner to intermediate level. Also, this section is helpful to instructors, for it will help them filter what information should be conveyed when initially teaching this form to others.

Advanced Information

This section will summarize the information for which an advanced practitioner should be aware. It is intended for the advanced practitioners and instructors. It covers some of the lesser known information related to Short Form One.

Reverse / Opposite Analysis

This section will collate and expose the reverse / opposite information presented in the form. This is important because, by definition, American Kenpo forms give an example of reverses and opposites. This section is intended to help simplify this analysis by exposing the reverses and opposites for each section of the form.

Principles / Rules / Theories / Concepts / Definitions

This section will list the terms related to Short Form One. Each term will need to be further researched by the reader. This section is provided mainly as a starting point into further analysis of American Kenpo terminology, concepts, theories, rules, and principles.

Beginning / Intermediate Analysis

Short Form One introduces:

1)

    The definition of a kenpo form:
      A predefined series of maneuvers that:
        a) show the rules and principles of motion,
        b) that everything has a reverse and an opposite,
        c) by giving an example

2)

    The concept that each form has footwork. This sets the concepts that the practitioner must learn:
      a) to coordinate the basic timing between their upper and lower body
      b) to keep their feet on the ground - unless kicking, stomping, etc.
      c) to remove extra motions from their footwork. This sets the concepts of:
        i) no breaking of the heel
        ii) no pivoting on the heel
      d) not to lean while executing maneuvers. This sets the concepts:
        i) no jet lagging
        ii) leaning disrupts smooth rotation of the body for blocking
      e) to maintain a relatively constant head height while executing maneuvers
      f) to maneuver into proper stances
      g) to move as efficiently as possible from stance to stance
      h) that one foot is used to transition from one stance to the next - not both (i.e. do not "split" a stance)
      i) to look before covering to a new direction
      j) steps should be as direct as possible to the new location, minimizing distance to new location. This sets the concept of:
        i) economy of motion

k) step-through maneuvers are distance with rotation - not distance then rotation
l) to create distance between you and your opponent

3)

The concept that each form is done from a standing stance. This sets the concepts that the practitioner must learn:
a) to keep their back straight at all times
b) the proper dimensions of each stance
c) to create a stable base

4)

The concept of defense - i.e. blocking. This sets the concepts that the practitioner must learn:
a) the definition of a block:
   i) force against force
   ii) against an offensive weapon in flight
   iii) without the intent to cause injury to the opponent
b) each block should be executed within their outer rim - i.e. invisible box
c) each block has a proper height, depth, and width execution
d) blocks have different methods of execution
e) blocks work on the power principle of torque
f) blocks intend to make contact with the forearm
g) blocks employ the '+' / 'x' rule
h) offensive weapons can come from the front, rear, or either side of the body
i) offensive weapons can come from the high, low, or middle height zones
j) double factoring. This sets the concepts that:
   i) the inward block is the double factor for high blocks, and therefore does not have a double factor
   ii) the inside downward, palm up block is the double factor for low blocks
   iii) the double factor is executed with the planting of the foot on the foot maneuver - the block is executed with the settle into the stance

     vi) double factors allow for more force to be
     delivered with the main block
    k) blocks should make contact with the offensive
    weapon at a proper distance from the intended point of
    contact on your body.

5)

    The concept that each form ends in an attention stance.

6)

    The concept that each form has a pattern or number of
    patterns that its execution creates. This form:
      a) creates the '+' pattern by facing the four major
      directions (12:00 - 3:00 - 6:00 - 9:00)
      b) creates an 'L' pattern with the actual foot maneuvers

7)

    The concept of staying relaxed and only tensing, for short
    periods of time, at the proper moment.

Short Form One falls into the category of a dictionary form. As
such, it introduces the following elements of the dictionary
forms.

1)

    The blocking sequence:
      a) In
      b) Out
      c) Up
      d) Down

2)

    Each form starts from the meditating horse stance.

Short Form One has a number of other elements it teaches:

1)
It is defined as follows:
a) it is a front hand only form
b) it is a defensive only form
c) it is a retreating only form

2)
The rear hand should always be chambered in-sync with the blocking hand. The reverse motion of the retracting arm then emphasizes and optimizes the power generated by the front arm.

3)
The first and last position of the form are identical - a meditating horse.

4)
The line of sight should be kept straight ahead and never upward or downward. This sets the concepts that:
a) you are always looking at your opponent
b) you never turn your back to your opponent

5)
Single beat timing

6)
Covering into the unknown retreats away from the opponent (i.e. creates distance)

7)
The following stances:
a) Meditating Horse
b) Neutral Bow

Advanced Analysis

Short Form One introduces:

1)

>   The concept that each form has footwork. This sets the
>   concepts that the practitioner must learn:
>   a) that settling into a stance enhances power
>   b) that the degrees of a cover to a new direction can
>   vary. In this case 180 degrees and 90 degrees.
>   c) weight shifting on 180 degree covers should be kept
>   to a minimum

2)

>   The concept that each form is done from a standing
>   stance. This sets the concepts that the practitioner must
>   learn:
>   a) that each stance has a purpose in application
>   b) that stances are designed to limit exposure to vital
>   targets
>   c) that stances are designed to NOT limit the
>   availability of the practitioners weapons

3)

>   The concept of defense - i.e. blocking. This sets the
>   concepts that the practitioner must learn:
>   a) blocks intend to create an Angle of Deflection
>   against an offensive weapon
>   b) blocks create a path of travel (as opposed to a line
>   of travel)
>   c) double factoring. This sets the concepts that:
>   i) blocks can be both minor and major moves
>   ii) the rear hand is used to fill gaps in timing
>   between blocks
>   iii) double factors protect the center-line and face

4)

>   The concept that each form has a predominant (or theme)
>   stance. In this case, the Neutral Bow.

5)

The concept of category completion.

6)

Each move in the form should be defined. This sets the concepts that:
- a) moves should NOT be mumbled together
- b) each move is a complete unit, even though it is part of a larger whole
- c) correct timing within a single move and between moves is critical

---

Short Form One falls into the category of a dictionary form. As such, it introduces the following elements of the dictionary forms.

1)

Each starts with a right hand inward hammering block. The key elements being:
- a) defensive first
    - i) this sets the concepts that:
        - 1) our system is a defensive system
        - 2) defense is more important than offense
- b) front hand first
    - i) this sets the concept that:
        - 1) the front hand is used for defense over the rear hand
- c) right hand first
    - i) this sets the concept that:
        - 1) our system is a right hand major system
- d) inward first
    - i) this sets the concept that:
        - 1) inward motion tends to be the predominant direction for defensive purposes.
- e) hammering method of execution first
    - i) this sets the concepts that:
        - 1) hammering is stronger than other defensive methods of execution

2) always employ the principle of economy of motion
3) hammering methods of execution are derived from a cocked position

2)

The second inward block uses a thrusting method of execution. This sets the concepts that thrusting methods of execution:
a) are derived from point of origin
b) always employ the principle of Economy of Motion
c) are faster than hammering methods of execution
d) travel less distance than hammering methods of execution

3)

Each dictionary form changes the foot pattern on the first downward block.

4)

Each dictionary form blocks with the vertical outward block, even though this block is considered obsolete and not used in the system. This motion is used for other purposes, but not as a block.

Short Form One has a number of other elements it teaches:

1)

It introduces the following types of Torque:
a) direct rotational
i) Inward block #1 & #2
ii) Outward block #1
iii) Downward block #1
b) counter rotational
i) Outward block #2
ii) Downward block #2
c) isolated
i) Upward block #1 & #2

2)

It shows that the blocks are executed in pairs with the following facts:

a) The first block of each blocking pair (with the exception of the first inward block) is executed to a new direction

b) The second block of each blocking pair is executed stepping backward while facing the same direction

c) Blocks do NOT always alternate hands between blocking pairs

d) The foot utilized in the foot maneuver is ALWAYS the opposite to the blocking arm

3)

The form assumes an open environment in which the practitioner can freely move in any direction away from the offensive weapons. This sets the concepts of:

a) Environmental Awareness

b) Environmental Consideration

c) Peripheral Awareness

4)

It shows that turning (180 degrees) into the unknown requires extra protection. It sets the concepts that:

a) the upward block provides the most protective cover (both the middle and upper height zones) of the blocks

b) the double factor provides an intersection (double) in which all of the other blocks may be executed - with either arm (because of the double intersection)

Reverse / Opposite Analysis

Note:
> This analysis is limited to only the basics contained in Short Form One. It does not include basics that are in future forms.

Blocks

Right Hammering Inward Block
    Reverses
        None
    Opposites
        Left Block
        Left Inward Block
        Thrusting Inward Block
        Outward Block

Left Thrusting Inward Block
    Reverses
        None
    Opposites
        Right Block
        Right Inward Block
        Hammering Inward Block
        Outward Block

Left Vertical Outward Block
    Reverses
        None
    Opposites
        Right Block
        Right Vertical Outward Block
        Inward Block
        Outside Downward Block

Right Vertical Outward Block
    Reverses
        None
    Opposites
        Left Block
        Left Vertical Outward Block
        Inward Block
        Outside Downward Block

Left Upward Block
    Reverses
        None
    Opposites
        Right Block
        Right Upward Block
        Downward Block

Right Upward Block
    Reverses
        None
    Opposites
        Left Block
        Left Upward Block
        Downward Block

Right (Outside) Downward Block
    Reverses
        None
    Opposites
        Left Block
        Left (Outside) Downward Block
        Upward Block
        Vertical Outward Block

Left (Outside) Downward Block
    Reverses
        None
    Opposites
        Right Block
        Right (Outside) Downward Block
        Upward Block
        Vertical Outward Block

Foot Maneuvers

Left Step Through Reverse
    Reverses
        None
    Opposites
        Right Step Through Reverse
        Cover

Right Step Through Reverse
    Reverses
        None
    Opposites
        Left Step Through Reverse
        Cover

Right 90 Degree Cover
    Reverses
        Left 90 Degree Cover
    Opposites
        Left 90 Degree Cover
        180 Degree Cover
        Step Through

Left 90 Degree Cover
    Reverses
        Right 90 Degree Cover
    Opposites
        Right 90 Degree Cover
        180 Degree Cover
        Step Through

Right 180 Degree Cover
    Reverses
        Left 180 Degree Cover
    Opposites
        Left 180 Degree Cover
        90 Degree Cover
        Step Through

Left 180 Degree Cover
   Reverses
      Right 180 Degree Cover
   Opposites
      Right 180 Degree Cover
      90 Degree Cover
      Step Through

Power

Counterclockwise Direct Rotational Force
> Reverses
>> Clockwise Direct Rotational Force
> Opposites
>> Clockwise Direct Rotational Force
>> Counter Rotational Force

Clockwise Direct Rotational Force
> Reverses
>> Counterclockwise Direct Rotational Force
> Opposites
>> Counterclockwise Direct Rotational Force
>> Counter Rotational Force

Counter Rotational Force – Body Clockwise / Arm Counter Clockwise
> Reverses
>> Counter Rotational Force – Body Counterclockwise / Arm Clockwise
> Opposites
>> Counter Rotational Force – Body Counterclockwise / Arm Clockwise
>> Direct Rotational Force

Counter Rotational Force – Body Counterclockwise / Arm Clockwise
> Reverses
>> Counter Rotational Force – Body Clockwise / Arm Counterclockwise
> Opposites
>> Counter Rotational Force – Body Clockwise / Arm Counterclockwise
>> Direct Rotational Force

Direction

12:00 -> 6:00
    Reverses
        6:00 -> 12:00
    Opposites
        6:00 -> 12:00
        3:00 -> 9:00
        9:00 -> 3:00

3:00 -> 9:00
    Reverses
        9:00 -> 3:00
    Opposites
        9:00 -> 3:00
        12:00 -> 6:00
        6:00 -> 12:00

9:00 -> 3:00
    Reverses
        3:00 -> 9:00
    Opposites
        3:00 -> 9:00
        12:00 -> 6:00
        6:00 -> 12:00

6:00 -> 12:00
    Reverses
        12:00 -> 6:00
    Opposites
        12:00 -> 6:00
        3:00 -> 9:00
        9:00 -> 3:00

Principles / Rules / Theories / Concepts / Definitions Analysis

Dictionary

Align, Angle, Attacker, Attention, Attitude, Available, Balance, Ball, Base, Bounce, Bow, Category, Center-line, Chamber, Circle, Cock, Concept, Contact, Coordination, Defense, Deflect, Deliver, Depth, Deviate, Diagonal, Dictionary, Dimension, Direct, Direction, Disharmony, Distance, Downward, Embryonic, Environment, Execute, Exhale, Focus, Force, Form, Forward, Front, Gap, Gauge, Guide, Hammer, Hard, Height, Hide, Hidden, Horizontal, Hurt, Idea, Inhale, Inside, Intent, Intentional, Intercept, Intersect, Inward, Isolation, Kata, Lever, Leverage, Line, Major, Maneuver, Mechanical, Meditation, Meet, Method, Minor, Motion, Move, Mumble, Neutral, Offense, Opponent, Opposite, Outer, Outward, Path, Pivot, Plane, Plant, Plus, Position, Posture, Power, Practice, Practitioner, Prevent, Primitive, Principle, Pronounce, Proportional, Protect, Range, Rank, Read, Rear, Redirect, Relax, Retract, Reverse, Rhythm, Rotate, Rule, Salutation, Saying, Scan, School, Sensei, Set, Settle, Shape, Side, Signify, Simultaneous, Slide, Soft, Solidify, Sophisticated, Space, Speed, Square, Stable, Stationary, Step, Strike, Student, Studio, Style, Survey, Switch, Symmetrical, Sync, Synchronize, System, Tactic, Tailor, Target, Telegraph, Theory, Thrust, Timing, Tip, Torque, Touch, Tournament, Traditional, Train, Transitory, Travel, Turn, Unify, Unuseful, Upward, Use, Velocity, Vertical, Viewpoint, Weapon, Width, With, Yield, Zone

Terms

8 Major Angles of Attack, 8 Major Angles of Balance, 8 Major Angles of Defense, Alphabet of Motion, Anatomical Positioning, Anatomical Weak Point, Angle Alignment, Angle of Attack, Angle of Avoidance, Angle of Balance, Angle of

Contact, Angle of Cover, Angle of Defense, Angle of Deflection, Angle of Delivery, Angle of Departure, Angle of Deviation, Angle of Efficiency, Angle of Execution, Angle of Prevention, Angle of Protection, Angle of Travel, Articulation of Motion, Axis of Rotation, Body Alignment, Body Harmony, Body Mechanics, Body Momentum, Body Rotation, Body Settle, Break the Heel, Broken Rhythm, Category Completion, Chambered Position, Changing the Guard, Circular Confinement, Clock Principle, Close the Gate, Close the Line, Colliding Forces, Conceptual Box, Contact Deviation, Corrective Adjustment, Defensive Defense, Defensive Reaction, Degree of Rotation, Delayed Movement, Depth of Action, Depth Perception, Depth Zone, Diagonal Plane, Dimensional Zone, Directional Harmony, Directional Movement, Directional Switch, Disharmony of Travel, Disharmony of Force, Disrupted Rhythm, Double Factor, Economy of Motion, Environmental Awareness, Environmental Condition, Establish your Base, Field of View, Filling the Gap, Fluid Movement, Form Indicator, Gauging Leg, General Rule, Geometric Angle, Geometric Line, Geometric Path, Harmonious Movement, Harmonized Power, Heel-Knee Alignment, Heel-Toe Alignment, Height Zone, Horizontal Plane, Horizontal Zone, Horizontal Zone of Attack, Horizontal Zone of Defense, Horizontal Zone of Protection, In Sync, Intersecting Action, Intersecting Forces, Invisible Box, Jet Lag, L Shaped pattern, Line of Action, Line of Attack, Line of Defense, Line of Delivery, Line of Execution, Line of Sight, Line of Travel, Maintain the Gap, Margin for Error, Mental Distraction, Mental Harmony, Method of Defense, Method of Delivery, Method of Execution, Method of Travel, Mirror Image, Motion Analysis, Natural Defenses, Natural Weapon, Neutral Zone of Defense, Open the Gap, Open the Gate, Open the Line, Opposing Forces, Opposite Motion, Outer Rim, Over Rotate, Path of Action, Path of Attack, Path of Defense, Path of Delivery, Path of Entry, Path of Execution, Path of Travel, Peripheral Assessment, Peripheral Awareness, Peripheral Registering, Peripheral Scan, Peripheral Vision, Physical Harmony, Physical Preparedness, Physical Speed, Pivot Point, Pivoting Axis, Point of Cancellation, Point of Contact, Point of Pivot, Point of Reference, Positional Alignment, Positional Cock, Positional Cover, Positioned Block, Postural Position,

Power Principle, Proportional Dimension, Proportional Execution, Protective Measure, Reference Point, Residual Torque, Reverse Motion, Rotating Axis, Rotating Force, Rotational Velocity, Self-correcting, Settle into Balance, Solidify your Base, Stabilize your Base, Step Back, Target Availability, Toe-Heel Alignment, Toe-Toe Alignment, Toe-Toe Heel-Heel Alignment, Total Harmony, Total Mental Harmony, Total Physical Harmony, Transitional Move, Useless, V Step, Vertical Plane, Visual Interpretation, Vital Area, Vital Target, Wasted Motion, Weapon Availability, Weight Distribution, Width Zone, Zone of Confinement, Zone of Protection

Chapter 8 - Improving Your Execution of Short Form One

There is a lot of subtle and often overlooked execution information that can be learned from Short Form One. The vast majority of this information is absorbed through perfecting the form through practice and through feedback from an instructor. Often this feedback and 'perfecting' is minute and absorbed through repetition and repeated correction. Also, this information is often absorbed over a long period of time, over a large number of practice sessions, and gets almost to the point that the information is absorbed subconsciously. To quote an often used phrase - 'One cannot fool experience'.

Also, perfecting the execution of the other American Kenpo forms can help improve the execution of Short Form One. Therefore, it is not recommended that the practitioner preclude the practice of the other forms for this one. The diverse movements of the other forms can and will help to improve the execution of the seemingly simplistic maneuvers of this form.

Even though Short Form One is a very basic form, the skilled eye can easily discern differences between practiced and knowledgeable executions, from those that are more primitive and/or less experienced. Timing, elimination of wasted motion, settling, power, and smooth execution are only some of the factors that comprise a properly executed form.

Following is a categorized list of errors that can be made during the execution of Short Form One.

General Errors

a) improper timing:
    i) double factor is not executed with initial foot contact of maneuver
    ii) major block is not timed with the settle into stance

b) not turning head to new direction prior to foot maneuver

c) not looking straight ahead – i.e. looking up, down or wondering eyes

d) improper breathing:
    i) holding breath
    ii) breathing in during execution of major blocks

Timing

Timing is the coordination of multiple movements such that they are synchronized as intended. This definition is demonstrated throughout the form by timing both foot maneuvers (lower body) with blocks (upper body) in such a way as to create harmonious and fluid maneuvers which complete their execution in-sync with one another. With experience and practice, one can easily see correctly timed maneuvers from incorrectly timed maneuvers.

Gaze

The look on a practitioner's face and specifically the look in their eyes can heavily influence the perception of how a form is perceived. It is said that the eyes are the window to the soul. One can use this adage to their advantage to manipulate the viewer's perception of one's performance. This along with the practitioner's attitude can go a long way to overcoming other short-falls that may occur in their form execution.

During the execution of Short Form One, the practitioner should always keep their gaze at eye level and parallel to the floor. This practice helps in maintaining a straight back and well balanced stance. Also, it is a general rule to always look into the direction one is intending to step before executing the foot maneuver. This should be done by not only shifting the eyes, but also turning the head.

Breathing

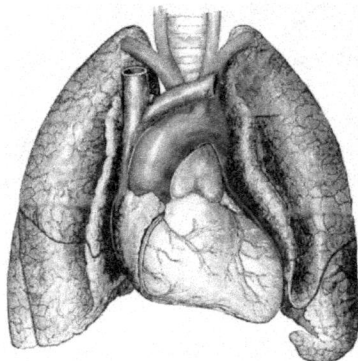

Breathing is an important part of the execution of any maneuver in American Kenpo. Short Form One is no exception. One must learn the importance of breath and how it affects their performance.

One bad habit that numerous beginner to intermediate students sometimes pick up is the holding of their breath during the execution of maneuvers. This should be corrected by having the practitioner concentrate on smooth and relaxed breathing. The only emphasis in one's breath should be at the anticipated point of contact of the block. This emphasis of breath should be for the purpose of helping to focus one's energy. Holding one's breath can lead to Constipated Motion - i.e. motion that is not fluid and/or smooth, but rather staccato and/or stiff in nature.

The kiai is a form of focusing one's breath by creating an audible sound with the breath through tightening of the abdominal muscles, thus forcing the breath to exhale. Some instructors teach using kiais to help students focus their breath with their maneuvers. Although Short Form One does not specifically contain any kiais in it's standard execution, it is not an incorrect nor bad teaching tool. On the contrary, it can be used to help a student correct breathing issues, along with teaching the purpose of tightening muscles in anticipation of absorbing an oncoming strike to the body. It can also be used as an 'attention getter' when executing a form in competition.

Stances

Stances are the base of our execution. Stances can be loosely defined as frozen motion. Without properly articulated stances, the execution of Short Form One can never be perfected. The most commonly overlooked item among stances is proper positioning. Positioning includes a large number of elements. These include foot/leg alignments, body alignments, and arm/hand alignments. One should become comfortable with the knowledge of proper alignments and dimensions of the stances. This cannot be overstated. The proper dimensions and alignments of each of the stances is highlighted in detail in SGM Parker's book, "Infinite Insights into Kenpo - book #2 (Physical Analyzation I)."

Short Form One, being the first form of the system, exposes only two stances during it's execution (not including the salutation): the Meditating Horse and the Neutral Bow.

Some of the most common mistakes of the Neutral Bow are: not having both feet point forward at 45 degree angle; not having the proper width (toe / heel alignment) or depth (heel / knee alignment), uneven weight distribution (50% / 50%), and/ or not keeping the back up straight with the shoulders relaxed.

Some of the most common mistakes of the Meditating Horse are: not having the toes point directly ahead (or slightly inward), not bending the knees, not having both elbows point downward at a 45 degree angle, and/or not keeping the back up straight.

It is very common for the practitioner to start out with proper alignments, but quickly lose the alignments once any foot maneuvers are executed. One good exercise for drawing attention to the stances is to perform the entire form without the blocks and with hands on the hips. This exercise allows the practitioner to pay exclusive attention to the stances and foot maneuvers without having to split their attention on proper block execution.

Stance Errors

a) general:
    i) improper alignments (see below)
        1) foot width improper
        2) foot depth improper
        3) height improper (knees not bent enough or too much)
    ii) improper rotation for stance
        1) both feet not facing same direction
        2) body and feet not facing same direction
    iii) improper weight distribution
    iv) leaning in stance

b) meditating horse - (alignments = toe/toe – heel/heel) (rotation – straight forward)
    i) stepping out with the right foot instead of the left
    ii) hands not at proper height (chest to chin level)

c) neutral bow - (alignments = toe/heel – heel/knee) (rotation – forward at 45 degrees)

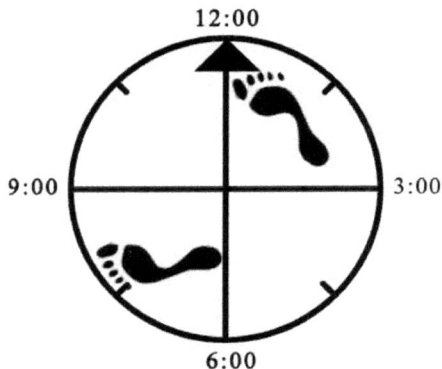

Example of bad rear foot angle for Neutral Bow

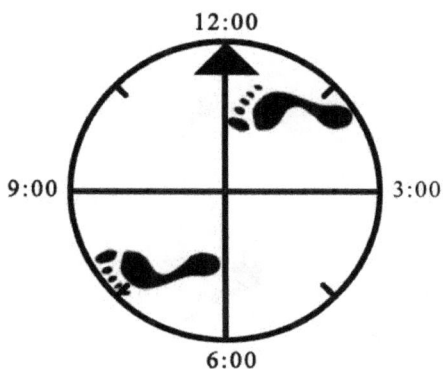

Example of bad foot angles (both) for Neutral Bow

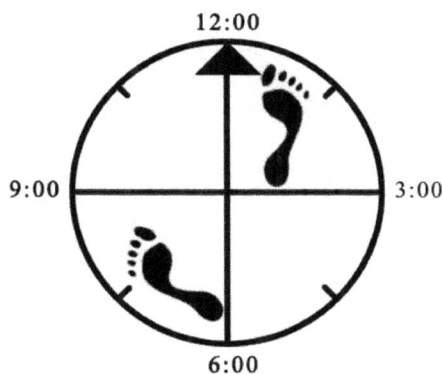

Example of bad front foot angle for Neutral Bow

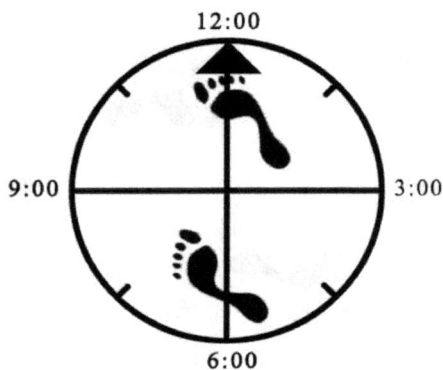

Example of improper width (narrow) for Neutral Bow

Foot Maneuvers

Foot maneuvers are basically the movement between stances. The improper execution of foot maneuvers can introduce a number of complexities of not only the movement itself, but also affect the new stance that is obtained at the end of the foot maneuver. The section on stance correction gives further highlights into this information.

There are a number of common errors exhibited while executing foot maneuvers. Bobbing is one of the most common problems demonstrated by many beginning practitioners. Transitions between stances should be fluid while also maintaining the same height level. Once Short Form One is started, the practitioner's head should remain at the same level throughout the entire execution of the form (including the Meditating Horse).

Another common general error is extra motions, i.e. breaking the principle of Economy of Motion. This problem is exhibited in many forms, the most common of which are: moving the feet prior to actually executing the foot maneuver (extremely common), breaking the heel (lifting the heel) during step through maneuvers, pivoting on the heel of the foot, and/or Jet Lagging (leaning while stepping through).

Note: The FAQ section has further discussion on the problems associated with rotating on the heel of the foot.

Foot Maneuver Errors

a) not obeying Economy of Motion principle / Create a stable base rule
- i) creating too many adjustments with feet
    - 1) breaking the heel (lifting/moving rear of foot before moving front of foot)
    - 2) adjusting/rotating feet prior to/during foot maneuvers
    - 3) adjusting the foot not used in a foot maneuver
    - 4) re-adjusting foot used in foot maneuver, after maneuver
- ii) foot not stepping directly to new location
- iii) splitting the stance (moving both feet, instead of one)
- iv) bouncing up and down while executing foot maneuver or stationary

b) improper pivoting:
- i) rotating on the heel instead of the ball of the foot
- ii) executing a twist through instead of a step through (splitting timing of distance/rotation during foot maneuver)

c) jet legging (splitting timing of lower/upper body – i.e. creating distance with feet first and then the upper body)

d) executing a cat stance as a separate motion – i.e. holding cat stance too long

Example of bobbing during a step through, reverse

Blocks

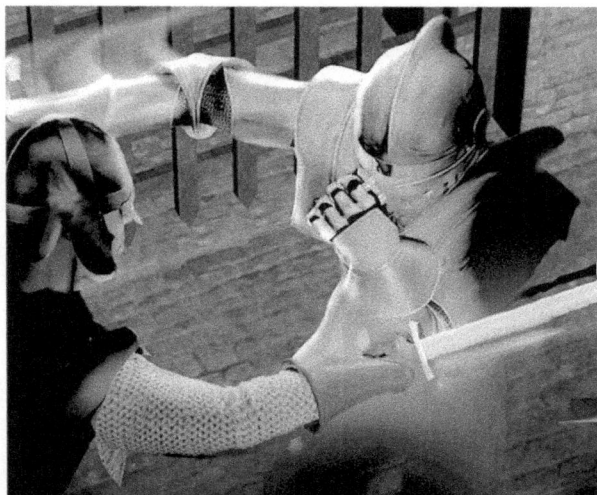

Blocking (defense) is the major theme of Short Form One. Executing the blocks properly can make the difference between a successful defense and failure. Just like the stances, the practitioner should become intimately familiar with the proper dimensions utilized in each of the blocks. The primary concepts in dealing with blocking dimensions are the Outer Rim theory and/or the Invisible Box theory. These theories along with the proper dimensions for each block are highlighted in detail in SGM Parker's book, "Infinite Insights into Kenpo, book #3 (Physical Analyzation II)."

Some of the most common mistakes displayed while executing Short Form One are: not executing the blocks to the proper dimensions; not executing the blocks to the proper angles; not executing the double factor block properly (especially the upward block); not executing the blocks efficiently (without Economy of Motion); and/or executing the block with improper timing.

Note: The FAQ section has further discussion on double factor blocks and their importance to Short Form One.

Block Errors

a) not obeying Economy of Motion principle
    i) making a cock before execution of block
    ii) executing blocking outside the outer rim/invisible box
    iii) chamber motion for downward block done too high
    (face height instead parallel to ground)

b) not obeying the rule of Margin for Error
    i) upward block done like chicken wings, no torque, just
    arm lifting
    ii) not anchoring the elbow on vertical outward blocks
    iii) not keeping the vertical outward block vertical – i.e.
    over reaching

c) improper alignments:
    i) inward block
        1) not at eye-brow level
        2) not extended to opposite shoulder
        3) not extended to proper depth
        4) execution angle not forward at 45 degrees
    ii) vertical outward block
        1) not at eye-brow level
        2) not extended to same shoulder
        3) palm not facing direct toward you
    iii) upward block
        1) not ending with angle of deflection
        2) not raising block to proper height
        3) not extending block to opposite shoulder
        4) not ending with fist positioned (palm facing directly
        forward) forward at 45 degrees away from you
    iv) downward
        1) not parallel to front knee after execution
        2) not extended to same shoulder
        3) palm not facing straight downward
        4) 'locking out' elbow during and after execution of
        block

d) double factors:
    i) crossing center line with upward block double factor

ii) not crossing center line with vertical outward double factor
iii) downward block double factoring not executed palm up (instead palm down)

e) executing two hammering inward blocks (instead of a hammering and thrusting)

f) hand is not completely closed when executing blocks (minor and/or major)

g) not executing the blocks smoothly - i.e. mechanical / staccato motion

Examples of bad Inward Blocks
(improper angle, width, and height - high / low)

Examples of bad outward Blocks
(improper width, angle, and shrugged shoulders)

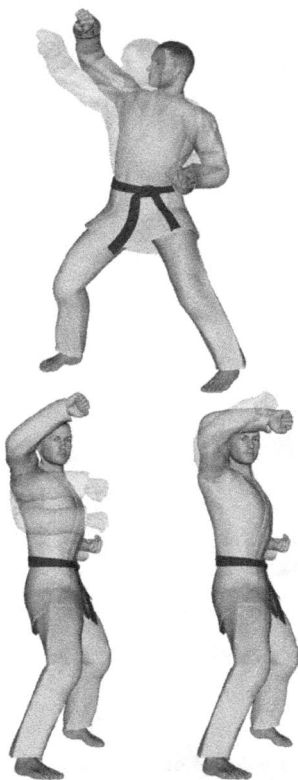

**Examples of bad upward Blocks
(leaning, improper transition, and
improper angle)**

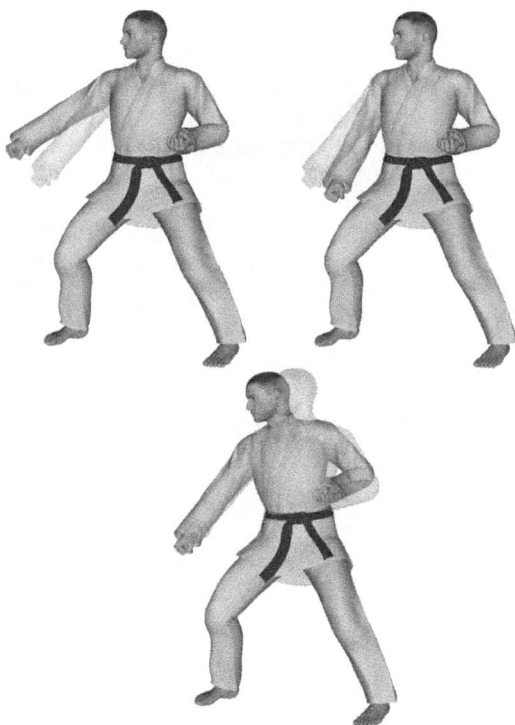

Examples of bad Downward Blocks
(improper height - high / low and leaning)

Improvement Priorities

The following chart is designed to help the practitioner correct the errors illustrated in this section. It provides the practitioner with a chart that maps the commonality of errors against the severity of errors.

To start fixing errors in short form one, start with the errors in the upper right hand corner and work downward and to the left of the graph. This will ensure the most sever errors and common errors are fixed first.

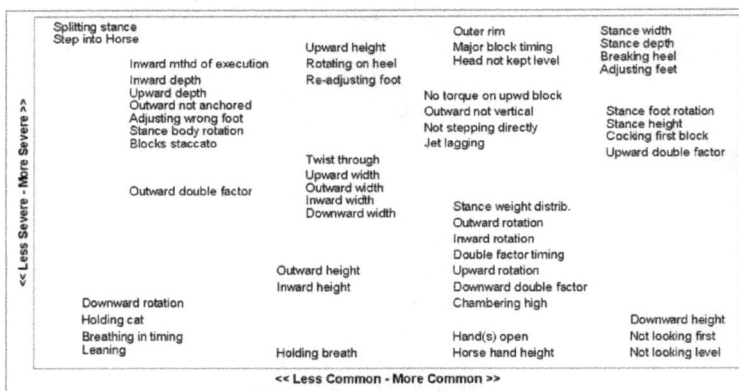

<< Less Severe - More Severe >>				
Splitting stance Step into Horse			Outer rim	Stance width Stance depth Breaking heel Adjusting feet
		Upward height Rotating on heel Re-adjusting foot	Major block timing Head not kept level	
	Inward mthd of execution Inward depth Upward depth Outward not anchored Adjusting wrong foot Stance body rotation Blocks staccato		No torque on upwd block Outward not vertical Not stepping directly Jet lagging	Stance foot rotation Stance height Cocking first block Upward double factor
	Outward double factor	Twist through Upward width Outward width Inward width Downward width	Stance weight distrib. Outward rotation Inward rotation Double factor timing	
		Outward height Inward height	Upward rotation Downward double factor Chambering high	
Downward rotation Holding cat Breathing in timing Leaning		Holding breath	Hand(s) open Horse hand height	Downward height Not looking first Not looking level
<< Less Common - More Common >>				

Chapter 9 - Frequently Asked Questions

This section highlights information presented in other sections of this guide, but presents it in a question and answer format. One of the things the Q&A format allows for is presenting information from a different perspective. This perspective change can sometimes allow the reader to more quickly and firmly grasp the presented information. It also can combine information across multiple areas of the guide together. Thus, allowing the reader to understand connections that are not as obvious as in other formats.

What is the Definition of Short Form One?

It is said that everything in American Kenpo has a definition.
Therefore, Short Form One must have a definition. Its
definition is:
Short Form One is the first form in the American Kenpo system
which is distinguishable by the fact that it is a 1) defense only,
 2) retreating only, and 3) front hand only form.

We are taught Short Form One on both sides in my studio. Why does this guide only illustrate the form on the Right Side?

Learning and executing Short Form One on both sides is fine, but is not necessary from a system perspective. The opposite side (the left side) is already presented in the second half of Long Form One (during the triple block section), and therefore is not needed – again from a system point of view. The practice of doing the left side of Short Form One has been around for a long time. It originated for tournament competition, in order to make the form longer and in an attempt to get better scoring from the officiating judges.

Why does Short Form One start with a Right, Hammering, Inward block?

The answer can be broken down into the three parts of the question:

1) Right
The reason the first block of Short Form One is a right is because American Kenpo is a strong sided system. i.e. it takes advantage of your strong side (typically the right). And, Short Form One demonstrates this by making the first move of the first form a right handed maneuver.

2) Hammering
The reason the first block of Short Form One is hammering is two fold:
   a) Because the practitioners' right hand is already cocked from the meditating horse, and to obey the principle of Economy of motion, the best move would be a Hammering Method of Execution.

   b) Because Hammering is a stronger Method of Execution than Thrusting. For example, when first learning the inward block, the student is initially taught to cock the weapon before delivery (Hammering). Later the student is taught that the quicker Method of Execution from the Training Horse stance is Thrusting. i.e. from Point of Origin. This is for the same reason. To show the stronger Method of Execution for a beginning student.

3) Inward
The reason the Inward Block is the first block of Short Form One is because the most common and useful block is the Inward Block. And, Short Form One demonstrates this by making it the first move of the first form of the system.

Why is Short Form One a 'defense only' form?

Short Form One is the first form of the system. As such, it lays out the foundation on which all of the rest of the forms build. And, blocking is the most important element of a 'self-defense' system. In other words – one of the first things a beginning student should learn to do is defend themselves. Therefore, Short Form One is isolated to doing defensive maneuvers. This allows the practitioner to only concentrate on defensive positioning and maneuvering, without the added complications of offensive maneuvers.

Why is Short Form One a 'retreat only' form?

Short Form One is the first form of the system. As such, it lays out the foundation on which all of the rest of the forms build. And, retreating away from an oncoming attack is the safest response for a beginning practitioner. Advancing into an attack is demonstrated in Long Form One only once, but both Short Form Two and Long Form Two are both executed almost exclusively advancing into the attack.

Why are all the blocks done with the front hand only?

Short Form One is the first form of the system. As such, it lays out the foundation on which all of the rest of the forms build. And, blocking with the front hand is the quickest and strongest method of blocking. Later (in Long Form One), blocking with the rear hand is added to show an opposite to blocking with the front hand.

Why is the block pattern/order chosen to be in, out, up, down?

Inward first, because inward is the most commonly used defensive maneuver. Next outward, because outward is the opposite of inward. Next upward, because the first Upward Block is done with a 180 degree cover; demonstrating, how to step off the line of attack and gain distance from the unknown – aka your Obscure Zone (behind you). Finally downward, because downward is the opposite of upward.

Why is only the neutral bow utilized in this form?

Short Form One is the first form of the system. As such, it lays out the foundation on which all of the rest of the forms build. And, the Neutral Bow stance is the 'work' stance and most common stance of the system. Therefore, it is highlighted as the 'theme' stance of Short Form One.

What importance does pivoting on the ball of the foot hold?

Pivoting on the ball of the foot allows the practitioner to eliminate extra (and unnecessary) motions during foot maneuvers. In a Neutral Bow stance, pressure is placed upon three primary points on the bottom of each foot. Two (2) on the ball of the foot (inside and outside of the ball), and one (1) on the rear of the foot (the heel). As the practitioner advances in skill the stance becomes more and more like a boxer's stance, where most weight is placed upon the ball of the foot, and not the heel. This positioning allows the practitioner to absorb more impact from the opponent(s).

For example: anyone familiar with boxing should have heard of the phrase - 'getting caught flat footed'. This phrase refers to the fact that the boxer got hit while their feet where flat on the floor - causing the boxer to not absorb and dissipate as much of the opponent's punching power as would be if their weight was kept primarily on the balls of the feet. This scenario usually occurs later in a fight, when the boxer becomes tired and can no longer keep minimal to no pressure on their heels.

If one maintains their stance with more weight towards the balls of their feet (as they should), rotating on the heels becomes a more difficult and timely ordeal. One must first shift their weight to the heel, pick up the ball of the foot, rotate the foot, replant the ball of the foot, and re-place the weight to the ball of the foot. But, if one rotates on the ball of the foot from the proper positioning, it is a simple matter to slide the heel to the new angle needed for the intended foot maneuver. Thus, removing a large number of steps, and getting closer to implementing full Economy of Motion (i.e. removing all wasted motion).

How should I breathe while performing this form?

One's breathe should be relatively smooth during the execution of Short Form One. The only emphasis on breath should be at the focus points of each block. This emphasis of breath will help in the timing and focus of the blocks - and contribute to achieving Harmonious Movement.

Why should I use double factor blocks?

Perfecting the use double factor blocks during the execution of Short Form One shows a more advanced and sophisticated understanding and mastery of motion. Often, Short Form One is taught without double factoring. But, double factoring is added as the practitioner becomes more adept at Short Form One's execution. Adding double factor blocks not only adds a layer of complexity to the form, but also: fills in timing gaps between blocks, helps improve execution timing, and introduces the concept of minor and major in defensive maneuvers.

It should also be noted that double factors are not officially considered part of the form, but rather a more sophisticated execution of the base form. If double factor blocks were considered part of the form, the definition of Short Form One would have to be changed to remove the "front hand only" section.

Why shouldn't we visualize an opponent while executing this form?

Visualizing an opponent is a good mental exercise for learning how to focus a maneuver to a specific point in space. By visualizing, one can pretend to be blocking an incoming attack, giving the blocks more urgency and focus. But, as in all American Kenpo forms, there is no intention for there to be an imaginary opponent. Rather, that the form demonstrates: the rules and principles of motion, that everything has a reverse and an opposite, and gives and example. Visualizing an opponent can detract from this goal and lead the practitioner into treating the form as a preordained imaginary fight, rather than a demonstration of motion study and analysis.

If I'm not visualize an imaginary opponent, where and what should I look at when doing the form?

When executing Short Form One, the practitioner should keep their gaze at eye level and parallel to the floor at all times.

How does leaning affect me?

Leaning can be done in a number of ways. First, one can just lean while settled in a stance (leaning); or, one can lean while maneuvering between stances (jet lagging). Either way, the back is not kept perpendicular to the ground.

In the case of a settled stance, leaning can decrease both the stability of a stance and decrease maneuverability of the stance. A straight back places the weight and position of the body in the center of the stance, i.e. the Intersection Position. From the Intersection Position it is more efficient to go in any possible direction. Also, when leaning it is easier for the attacker to make the defender go in one direction over another, because the defender's body is already positioned favoring a direction, which can be exploited.

In the case of maneuvering between stances, leaning creates precession. Precession is the wobble of a rotation that is not perfectly aligned vertically with its axis. For example the earth has a precession in its rotation. A precession, in this case, creates inefficiencies in rotation, breaking the principle of Economy of Motion. Also, leaning can create Jet Lagging. Jet Lagging is created by allowing the head and upper body to follow the lower body (instead of with the lower body) while stepping through in reverse. Since the purpose of stepping away is to create distance, letting the upper body lag behind the lower body exposes the face to the opponent for a longer period of time than necessary – creating a defensive problem, which can be exploited by the opponent.

154

| 152 | The Official EPAKS Guide to Short Form One |

Why is the form done in the "+" instead of another pattern?

The plus '+' pattern is the most simplistic pattern presented in American Kenpo forms. It contains the most basic opposite elements: front - back and left - right. Put together, these opposites form the plus '+' pattern. Also, this pattern lays out the two (2) major lines and the four (4) major angles for American Kenpo: 12:00 - 6:00 line and 9:00 - 3:00 line. Later forms begin to use the remaining minor lines: 10:30 - 4:30 line and 1:30 - 7:30 line.

© 2014 EPAKS Publications

If this form is for someone just starting, a beginner, why does it have so much information?

All American Kenpo forms contain an abundance of information. This is due to the fact that all American Kenpo forms, by definition, are designed to demonstrate information present in the system - and are not preordained, imaginary fights. But, as in all information contained in American Kenpo, it is designed to be absorbed over a long period of time. For example, a beginning student might not be expected to understand the different types of torque displayed in Short Form One. But, the beginner would most likely be expected to understand a lot of the opposite information contained in the form. But, as the practitioner continues to progress in American Kenpo, this information would be expected to be learned and absorbed at some point in their training.

Because of this layering of information, in American Kenpo, it is not only important to be able to execute the form properly; but as the practitioner becomes more and more advanced, it is expected that they also begin to understand more and more about the information presented in each form. And, that the practitioner also be able to explain this information in ever increasing detail, upon request.

What are the different types of torque used in Short Form One?

Torque is the 'theme' Power Principle of Short Form One. And, Short Form One demonstrates the three major forms of Torque - 1) Direct Rotational Torque, 2) Counter-Rotational Torque, and 3) Isolated Torque.

An example of Direct Rotational Torque can be found with the Inward Blocks. An example of Counter-Rotational Torque can be found with the second Vertical Outward Block. An example of Isolated Torque can be found with the Upward Blocks.

What Method of Execution types are used in Short Form One?

There are two Methods of Execution used in Short Form One - Hammering and Thrusting. An example of Hammering can be found with the first inward block of the form. An example of Thrusting can be found with the second inward block of the form.

Did SGM Parker create Short Form One?

He did not create the form initially. It is was what he referred to as an 'old' form. Meaning some similar manner of it existed prior to his formalizing American Kenpo. Some of the other forms that are considered 'old' are: Short Form 2, Finger Set, and Two Man Set.

What is meant by a 'dictionary' form?

Dictionary forms (i.e. Short Form One, Long Form One, Short Form Two, Long Form Two) concentrate more on 'defining' motion over theories and concepts. The 'encyclopedia' forms (i.e. the higher forms), rely more heavily on theories and concepts. While the 'appendix' forms (i.e. the sets) rely on concentrated information about a subject (i.e. kicking, blocking, finger strikes, etc.).

Are there elbow strikes hidden in Short Form One?

The quick answer - no. The long answer - some instructors have taught their students to execute back elbow strikes along with the blocks. This was done initially as a teaching aid, to ensure the student cocked their arm completely into a chambered position. Over time and generations of teaching, some people assumed that the 'elbows' were part of Short Form One, and began teaching Short Form One with this information included. Due to the definition of Short Form One (see other sections), there can be no strikes in the form.

Chapter 10 - Quizzes

This section contains quizzes that can be used to test one's understanding of Short Form One. They are designed to be used by the reader themselves, or by an instructor to query a student's understanding of the information presented in Short Form One. There are two groups of tests presented: 1) beginner to intermediate and 2) advanced. And, each group is broken down into two types of tests: 1) multiple choice and 2) fill in the blank.

The answers to each of the quizzes can be found in Appendix A at the back of this guide.

Multiple Choice - Beginner / Intermediate

1) How many blocks are executed in Short Form One (right side only)?
   a) 6
   b) 8
   c) 12
   d) There are no blocks in Short Form 1
   e) none of the above

2) The first move in Short Form One is:
   a) step back with your right leg while blocking with your left arm
   b) step back with your left leg while blocking with your right arm
   c) step back with your right leg while blocking with your right arm
   d) step back with your left leg while blocking with your left arm
   e) none of the above

3) The block sequence in Short Form One is:
   a) out, in, down, up
   b) up, in, out, down
   c) in, out, up, down
   d) down, up, out, in
   e) none of the above

4) Short Form One starts from a:
   a) Neutral bow stance
   b) Forward bow stance
   c) Cat stance
   d) Mediating horse stance
   e) none of the above

5) Short Form One is a:
   a) Dictionary form
   b) defense only form
   c) front hand only form
   d) all of the above
   e) none of the above

6) The pattern created by executing Short Form One is a(n):
   a) "T"
   b) "X"
   c) "Y"
   d) "+"
   e) "E"

7) The primary power principle of Short Form One is:
   a) Torque
   b) Back-up mass
   c) Gravitational marriage
   d) all of the above
   e) none of the above

8) Which stance is NOT part of Short Form One?
   a) Reverse Bow
   b) Forward Bow
   c) Cat
   d) all of the above
   e) none of the above

9) Your gaze should remain in which direction during the execution of Short Form One?
   a) upward
   b) downward
   c) straight ahead
   d) to your left
   e) to your right

---

10) Short Form One teaches you to stay:
    a) relaxed
    b) alert
    c) in sync
    d) all of the above
    e) none of the above

---

11) Extra movements in Short Form One:
    a) are welcome
    b) are necessary
    c) are done as needed
    d) are done to make the form longer for competition
    e) should be removed

---

12) The weight distribution during the blocks of Short Form One should be:
    a) equally distributed
    b) primarily to the front
    c) primarily to the rear
    d) primarily on the blocking foot
    e) always on the right foot

---

13) Stepping in Short Form One should be done:
  a) as deep as one can step
  b) with distance then rotation
  c) maintaining proper stance alignments
  d) after the block
  e) all of the above

14) The back elbows of Short Form One:
  a) are hidden
  b) are done to the person behind you
  c) there are no back elbows in sf1
  d) are done with the blocks
  e) none of the above

15) All foot maneuvers in Short Form One should be done with:
  a) both feet
  b) only the front foot
  c) only the stepping foot
  d) depends upon the foot maneuver
  e) none of the above

16) Leaning should be done:
  a) on all blocks
  b) only on the upward blocks
  c) only on the downward blocks
  d) always with the front hand
  e) never

17) Pivoting in foot maneuvers should be done:
   a) on the heel
   b) on ball of foot
   c) flat footed
   d) none of the above
   e) depends upon the foot maneuver

18) The imaginary opponent(s) in Short Form One:
   a) keeps moving
   b) stays in one spot
   c) there are more than one of them
   d) use both hands and feet
   e) there are no imaginary opponents

19) We step backward into a neutral bow in Short Form One to:
   a) create distance
   b) establish a stable base
   c) close our center line
   d) all of the above
   e) none of the above

20) The meditating horse stances of Short Form One:
   a) are only to open and close the form
   b) there are no meditating horse stances
   c) are used to create or close distance
   d) are used to create a stable base
   e) have no purpose

21) The points of the clock you look at during Short Form One are:
a) 10:30, 1:30, 3:00, 4:30
b) 12:00, 9:00, 3:00, 6:00
c) 6:00, 3:00, 10:00, 2:00
d) 10:30, 1:30, 4:30, 7:30
e) none of the above

22) The primary foot maneuver used in Short Form One is:
a) step thru forward
b) twist through reverse
c) step thru reverse
d) step-drag forward
e) none of these

23) What direction should your blocking forearm be facing during Short Form One:
a) to the side
b) forward
c) depends upon the block
d) downward
e) upward

24) Where should your non-blocking hand be placed during Short Form One:
a) checking forward
b) checking backward
c) hanging at your side
d) chambered at your side
e) covering your face

25) What direction should your feet face during Short Form
One:
    a) to the side
    b) to the back
    c) forward at a 45 degree angle
    d) straight ahead
    e) front foot towards the front, rear foot towards the back

Fill in the Blank - Beginner / Intermediate

1) Short Form One is the _____ form in the system.

2) The primary stance in Short Form One is the _____ bow.

3) The first block of Short Form One is the _____ inward block.

4) The second block of Short Form One is the _____ inward block.

5) The last block of Short Form One is the _____ downward block.

6) All blocks in Short Form One are executed with the _____ arm.

7) Short Form One is a(n) _____ only form.

8) All foot maneuvers in Short Form One _____.

9) Short Form One faces _____ directions.

10) The second pair of blocks in Short Form One are the
_____ outward blocks.

_____

11) Short Form One starts from a(n) _____ horse stance.

_____

12) Short Form One ends in a(n) _____ horse stance.

_____

13) The arm not blocking in Short Form One should be in
_____.

_____

14) There are _____ Methods of Execution demonstrated in
Short Form One.

_____

15) Stances are designed to create a stable _____ in Short
Form One.

_____

16) Vertical Outward Blocks that aren't vertical lose some
_____ for Error.

_____

17) The foot maneuver to switch directions in Short Form One
is called a(n) _____.

_____

18) The second block of each blocking pair is executed to the
same _____.

_____

19) Short Form One teaches you to pivot on the _____ of your foot.

_____

20) Adjusting your foot prior to a foot maneuver breaks the principle of _____ of Motion.

_____

21) The opposite of inward is _____.

_____

22) The first 180 degree cover is done on the first _____ block.

_____

23) All of the blocks are designed to make contact with your _____ against any incoming attacks.

_____

24) All the blocks of Short Form One should be executed with your hands _____.

_____

25) You should not hold your _____ during the execution of Short Form One.

Multiple Choice - Advanced

1) The step through foot maneuver creates:
   a) distance
   b) rotation
   c) Switch of side forward
   d) all of the above
   e) none of these

2) Which of these is NOT an opposite demonstrated in Short Form One?
   a) retreating / advancing
   b) in / out
   c) up / down
   d) left / right
   e) none of these

3) Short Form One teaches us the concept:
   a) height / width / Depth zones
   b) Outer rim
   c) Weight distribution
   d) Economy of Motion
   e) all of these

4) In Short Form One, how many moves demonstrate counter-rotational torque (right side only)?
   a) every move
   b) no moves
   c) one move
   d) two moves
   e) three moves

5) The opposite of direct rotational torque is:
    a) Back-up Mass
    b) Counter Rotational Torque
    c) Gravitational Marriage
    d) all of the above
    e) none of these

6) Why is the first upward block done with a 180 degree cover?
    a) to show that the upward double factor provides the most protection
    b) to maintain the plus '+' pattern of the form
    c) to move off the line of attack
    d) all of the above
    e) no reason

7) Double factor blocks:
    a) are minor blocks
    b) fill timing gaps
    c) are inward motion
    d) all of the above
    e) none of these

8) Settling into your stance:
    a) creates distance between you and your opponent
    b) plants your heels onto the ground
    c) moves you off the Line of Attack
    d) all of the above
    e) none of these

9) The concept of Margin for Error is demonstrated:
   a) in all of the blocks
   b) only on the inward and outward blocks
   c) only in the outward and downward blocks
   d) only on the outward blocks
   e) in none of the blocks

10) Which block does NOT create an Angle of Deflection?
    a) inward
    b) outward
    c) upward
    d) downward
    e) none of these

11) How many Methods of Execution are demonstrated in Short Form One?
    a) one
    b) two
    c) three
    d) all
    e) depends upon whether you do both sides

12) What is the actual foot pattern of Short Form One (right side only)?
    a) "X"
    b) "L"
    c) "+"
    d) "T"
    e) none of these

13) Short Form One starts with a right hammering inward block because:
   a) American Kenpo is a strong sided system
   b) the right hand is already cocked
   c) the inward block is the most effective and common block
   d) all of the above
   e) none of these

14) The environment in Short Form One is assumed to be:
   a) open
   b) closed
   c) filled
   d) all of the above
   e) none of these

15) Body Harmony is achieved through:
   a) breath
   b) timing
   c) body alignment
   d) all of the above
   e) none of these

16) What is the first principle introduced in Short Form One:
   a) windshield wiper
   b) centered mass
   c) gravitational marriage
   d) all of the above are introduced simultaneously
   e) none of the above

17) What is the first rule demonstrated in Short Form One:
   a) always keep your back straight
   b) don't make a cock a separate motion
   c) never split your stance
   d) all of the above are introduced simultaneously
   e) none of the above

18) There are no blocks with the rear arm because:
   a) they are introduced in Long Form One
   b) it is not as strong as the front
   c) we would have to shift into a forward bow
   d) takes too long
   e) it opens our center line

19) The vertical outward block of Short Form One:
   a) is better than the extended outward block
   b) is there to show the reverse line to the inward block
   c) should be done to meet the incoming strike
   d) all of the above
   e) none of the above

20) The inward block double-factors:
   a) are minor moves
   b) are outward blocks
   c) are done quicker than the others
   d) all of the above
   e) none of the above

21) The meditating horses of Short Form One are:
   a) not part of the form
   b) for meditation purposes
   c) only for the start of the dictionary forms
   d) all of the above
   e) none of the above

22) Who created Short Form One:
   a) its an old form
   b) SGM Ed Parker
   c) one of SGM Parker's students
   d) William K.S. Chow
   e) James Mitose

23) The perimeter of the outer rim is:
   a) head to toe - shoulder to shoulder
   b) head to groin - shoulder to shoulder
   c) chest to groin - along the center line
   d) sternum to toe - shoulder to shoulder
   e) head to sternum - along the center line

24) Breaking the heel:
   a) is supposed to be done with the rear foot
   b) should be avoided
   c) should only be done on the covers
   d) is a hidden foot maneuver
   e) helps rotation on the ball of the foot

25) Environmental awareness is shown by:
   a) turning your heard to the new direction
   b) stepping to the new direction
   c) the double factor blocks
   d) not cocking your blocking arm
   e) all of the above

Fill in the Blank - Advanced

1) The Hammering Method of Execution demonstrates _____ motion.

_____

2) The right outward and left outward blocks in Short Form One are _____(s) of each other.

_____

3) The first example of direct rotational torque in Short Form One is on the _____ inward block.

_____

4) The first example of counter rotational torque in Short Form One is on the _____ vertical outward block.

_____

5) The blocks of Short Form One create an Angle of _____.

_____

6) The blocks of Short Form One move on a _____ of Travel.

_____

7) Short Form One introduces the concept that American Kenpo is a _____ hand major system.

_____

8) The stepping foot in Short Form One is always the _____ to the blocking hand.

_____

9) There are _____ types of Torque demonstrated in Short Form One.

10) The double factor blocks of Short Form One are _____ blocks.

11) The _____ block is the double factor block for upper height zone.

12) The _____ arm is the primary defense arm of Short Form One.

13) The primary difference between a step through and a cover in Short Form One is _____.

14) Double factor blocks protect your _____.

15) Double factor blocks fill the _____(s) in timing.

16) Short Form One works on _____ in one timing.

17) Of the three types of forms in American Kenpo, Short Form One is classified as a(n) _____ form.

18) Short Form One shows that the _____ method of execution comes from a cocked position.

_____

19) Short Form One shows that the _____ method of execution comes from point of origin.

_____

20) The upward blocks in Short Form One use _____ torque.

_____

21) The hand positions of the meditating horse stance represent the _____ dynasty.

_____

22) The in,out,up,down sequence of Short Form One is an example of _____ completion.

_____

23) The purpose of the outer rim concept in Short Form One is to eliminate _____ motion.

_____

24) The _____ blocks show both hammering and thrusting Method of Execution.

_____

25) The _____ blocks can only be done with a hammering Method of Execution.

Appendix 1 - Quiz Answers

These are the answers to the quizzes presented earlier in the guide. The answer section order matches the quiz section order presented earlier.

Multiple Choice Answers - Beginner / Intermediate

1) b
2) b
3) c
4) d
5) e
6) d
7) a
8) d
9) c
10) d
11) e
12) a
13) c
14) c
15) e
16) e
17) d
18) e
19) d
20) a
21) b
22) c
23) c
24) d
25) c

Fill in the Blank Answers - Beginner / Intermediate

1) first
2) Neutral
3) Hammering
4) Thrusting
5) left
6) front
7) defense (or retreating) (or front hand)
8) retreat
9) four (4)
10) Vertical
11) Meditating
12) Meditating
13) chamber
14) two (2)
15) base
16) Margin
17) cover
18) direction
19) ball
20) Economy
21) outward
22) upward
23) forearm
24) closed
25) breath

Multiple Choice Answers - Advanced

1) d
2) a
3) e
4) d
5) b
6) d
7) d
8) e
9) a
10) e
11) b
12) b
13) d
14) a
15) d
16) e
17) d
18) a
19) e
20) a
21) d
22) a
23) b
24) b
25) a

Fill in the Blank Answers - Advanced

1) major
2) reverses (and opposites)
3) first
4) second (or left)
5) Deflection
6) Path
7) right
8) opposite
9) three (3)
10) minor
11) inward
12) front
13) distance
14) center-line
15) gaps
16) one (1)
17) Dictionary
18) Hammering
19) Thrusting
20) Isolated
21) Ming
22) Category
23) wasted
24) inward
25) downward

Appendix 2 - The Kenpo Kards

Kenpo Kards

The Kenpo Kards is a project by EPAKS that presents all of the American Kenpo self-defense techniques, forms, and sets to a quick reference card which can be used for study and entertainment. The Kenpo Kards were released in three (3) decks - beginner, intermediate, and advanced. Along with the Kards, EPAKS produced a guidebook to help in the usage of both the Kards and understanding of some of the foundational layout of American Kenpo.

Along with the physical version of the Kards and guidebook, EPAKS has released a digital version of each. The Kenpo Kards app is available on both the Google Play store and the Amazon App store. The digital guidebook is available on the Google Play store, the Amazon digital book store, and the Barnes and Noble digital book store.

The Kenpo Kard app allows the user to quickly sort and / or choose Kards to study, and allows for the user to play back the list for practicing alone or with up to five (5) partners. The app has options to select the speed to play the list, choose which yellow belt techniques to use in the sorting (old / new / both), and select the highest technique one has learned. This app is invaluable in helping to understand relations between techniques as well as to quickly group techniques by similarities - such as same attack, same side forward, same web of knowledge grouping, just to name a few.

One of the most important things the reader should understand is it is not the intent of the Kenpo Kards project to teach the practitioner how to do American Kenpo. Rather, it is to help the practitioner to explore and understand the information contained in the parts of the system they have learned from their instructor.

The Front of the Kard

The first thing one will notice about the front of the Kard is the signification of Short Form One. It is the most prominent image on the Kard. This layout is part of a theme that is shared among all of the Kards in the form Dek. As the forms increase in complexity, the signification becomes less prominent while at the same time the figures on the Kard become more prominent.

The next thing one should notice is that the figure on the Kard is executing the first move of Short Form One. This is part of another theme that is shared among all the Kards in the forms Dek. The figure and any other images (aside from the signification) will highlight the most important pieces of information and / or physical attributes of the form being illustrated. It is the intent that a person familiar with the form should be able to quickly ascertain which form is being illustrated without having to read the text.

The Back of the Kard

Short Form One

Ed Parker's American Kenpo System

CATEGORY
  Motion Definition (Dictionary)
PRIMARY THEMES
  Front hand only - Defense only - Retreating only
  Single Beat Timing
PRIMARY INTRODUCTIONS
  In-Out-Up-Down Blocking Series (Dictionary Forms)
  Rules and Principles of Motion
  Reverse / Opposite Category Completion
  Defense (Blocking)
  Upper / Lower Body Coordination
  Settling (to create Power) (Establish Base)
PRIMARY PRINCIPLES / THEORIES / CONCEPTS
  Economy of Motion
  Angle of Deflection
  Hammer / Thrust Methods of Execution
  Outer Rim (Invisible Box)
  Torque (Direct Rotational / Counter-Rotational / Isolated)
  Double Factor (Blocks)
  Environmental Awareness
  Environmental Consideration
  Peripheral Awareness
  Distance Gauging
  Path of Travel
PRIMARY MANEUVERS
  Step-Through Reverse (Left / Right)(Distance with Rotation)
  Cover (90⁰ / 180⁰) (Left / Right)

FS1   Rev. B/J   www.kenpokards.com   © Copyright 2010 EPAKS, Inc.

The back of the Kard can quickly be described as a microcosm of this guidebook. If you have read the book up to this point, the information presented on the Kard should be very easy to understand without much further explanation. What follows is a breakdown of the design and intent of the Kard.

The back of the Kard is divided into two columns. The left column is a textual summary of the major information presented in Short Form One. The right column is a quick overview of other attributes about Short Form One that are best or more quickly illustrated through images.

The Left Column

The left column lays out a quick overview of the major information presented in Short Form One. It should be noted that due to space limitations, not all information about Short Form One can be presented. So, a wide variety of the most important information has been included.

The left column is broken down into different 'categories of information.' This design is intended to help the practitioner in absorbing and comprehending the information in a more concentrated and targeted manner. In this way, the practitioner can be presented with related information that is presented in a concise manner, thereby enabling the practitioner to quickly overview a lot of information in a short period of time.

As stated earlier, the information illustrated on the back of the Kard is also presented in this guidebook - but in a more descriptive manner. It is suggested that the reader use this guidebook to help further research the information with which the reader is unfamiliar or needs more clarification and/or details.

The Right Column

The right column has three (3) rows.

1) The top row illustrates what category of form Short Form One falls into - in this case Dictionary (see Dictionary / Encyclopedia / Appendix analogy earlier in this book).

2) The middle row illustrates the theme stance of the form - in this case the Neutral Bow.

3) The bottom row lays out the important patterns of Short Form One - in this case the directional and foot patterns.

Index

- A -

- B -

- F -

- G -

- H -

- Q -

- T -

- U -

- V -

www.ingramcontent.com/pod-product-compliance
Lightning Source LLC
Chambersburg PA
CBHW072002090426
42740CB00011B/2056